Debbie Mumm's
Decorating with
Quick & Easy Quilts

Decorate your home with quilts you love!
From a French Country kitchen to a sophisticated
country-style living room, from a tropical sun room
to bedrooms brimming with flowers or campsite
comforts, you'll find lots of inspiration in the five
complete room environments in this book!
And, the more than thirty-five projects are so
quick and easy, you'll want to make them all!

DEBBIE
MUMM

dear friends,

One of my favorite ways to make a room warm, inviting, and filled with personal style is to decorate it with quilts! In this book, five distinctive rooms are filled with ideas for coordinated sewing projects...each with a designer look! Even better, we made sure that all of the projects fit our "quick and easy" criteria. You can count on speed piecing methods and innovative techniques to guide you quickly through these projects. You'll also find lots of inspiration for wall treatments, accessories, and easy decorating projects from the beautiful full color room-setting photographs.

We kept the projects as simple as possible by incorporating the following techniques~
~Repeating blocks to utilize quick
 assembly line methods.
~Fewer fabrics in each project to keep
 cutting simple.
~Larger pieces when appropriate.
~Innovative techniques – the project may
 look complex, but is still simple to make.
~Use of embellishments to add detail
 without lots of sewing time.
~Look for the 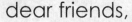 symbol for ways to
 make projects even easier!

Whichever rooms you are decorating, you'll find lots of quilting and decorating ideas throughout this book! So pour a cup of tea, get out your idea notepad, and be prepared to be inspired as you study the projects and rooms on these pages.

have fun & make it "quick & easy!"

Debbie Mumm

table of contents

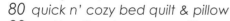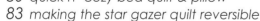

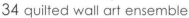

french country style

Wake up to the warmth of a French Country kitchen glowing with color and classic country themes. From the crowing rooster banner, to the fruit-filled curtains and tablecloth, to the mosaic fruit bowl, you'll find your own piece of the countryside in these pretty projects.

classic fruit bowl
framed quilt

Finished size: 34½" x 28½" with frame

With the intricate look of a mosaic and the sewing ease of stipple quilting, this beautiful fruit bowl will set the style for a French Country kitchen! A special product holds the pieces in place until you stipple the entire piece. Or, make it even easier by using whole fruit appliqués instead of the mosaic pieces.

fabric requirements & cutting instructions

Read all instructions before beginning.

Classic Fruit Bowl
MATERIALS NEEDED
Fabric A (Background) - ¾ yard   31" x 25" piece*
Fabric B (Tiles) - ⅙ yard   Thirty-six 1⅜ " squares
Fabric C (Tile Accent) - ⅛ yard   ¼" x 42" strip
Appliqués - Assorted scraps
Backing - ⅞ yard   35" x 29" piece
Batting - 35" x 29"
Frame - Inside measurement   27½" x 21½" (approximate)
Steam-a-Seam 2® Fusible Web -   1½ yards
Embroidery Floss - Green and   brown
Temporary Fabric Marker
* Adjust background size as needed to fit frame

getting started

We used Steam-A-Seam 2® double-stick fusible web. In addition to being fusible, this product has a pressure-sensitive coating on both sides that temporarily holds appliqués to background fabric, enabling you to reposition shapes before fusing. Read manufacturer's directions before beginning.

adding the appliqués

1. Using placement lines on pattern as guide, trace complete appliqué patterns (pages 9-13) on 27" x 21" paper. (You may need to tape several pieces of paper together to make complete pattern piece.)

Classic Fruit Bowl
Template Assembly

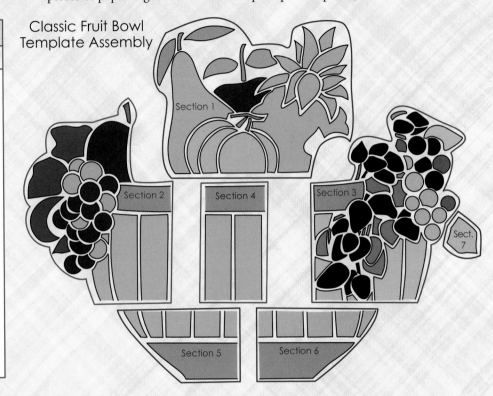

2. Center pattern and trace pattern lines on background fabric, using a light table or window and temporary marker to mark the pattern as shown in detail photo. Fabric piece is larger than shown.

3. Refer to manufacturer's directions then remove paper from one side of Steam-A-Seam 2®. Place wrong side of appliqué fabric onto Steam-A-Seam 2®. Apply pressure with hand to hold in place. Remove remaining paper.

4. Refer to photo and pattern on pages 6 and 7. To create mosaic effect, cut small pieces from several fabric scraps to fit within each element (e.g., each piece of fruit). Leave narrow spaces between pieces within design element, and wider spaces between motifs as shown. For each mosaic piece, place into position and apply pressure to temporarily stick in place.

5. Refer to photo on page 6 and layout below. Use Steam-A-Seam 2® and ¼"-wide strip of Fabric C to establish edge of tiles. If mosaic look is desired, use striped fabric for Fabric C. Round corners of thirty-six 1⅜" Fabric B squares for tiles. Arrange squares on background, trimming where needed to fit around bowl.

6. Reposition shapes until satisfied with placement. Following manufacturer's instructions, fuse appliqués to background.

layering & finishing

1. Arrange and baste backing, batting, and top together, referring to Layering the Quilt on page 110. Stipple quilt evenly over entire quilt surface to hold fused pieces securely.

2. Referring to photo on page 6 and Embroidery Stitch Guide on page 110, use three strands of embroidery floss and Stem Stitch to add tendrils to fruit and antennae to butterflies.

3. Refer to page 37, step 8, to install quilt in frame or to page 13, step 6, to bind quilt.

tip *For grapes, you may find it easier to trace circular shapes, then cut into pieces. Make a template of butterflies on page 12 and cut fabrics as shown.*

Section 2

Section 1

Classic Fruit Bowl Templates

Section 3

Tracing Line _____
Placement Line _ _ _ . _ _ _ .

Classic Fruit Bowl
Templates

Tracing Line _____
Placement Line _ _ _ _ _ _ _

Section 1

Section 2

Section 4

Section 5

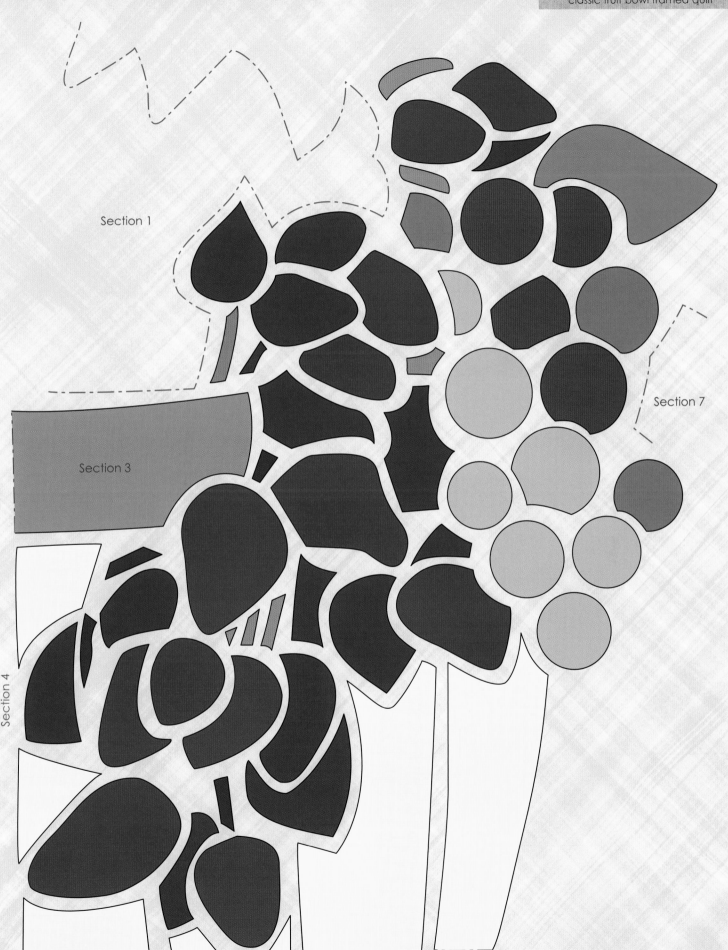

Section 1

Section 7

Section 3

Section 4

Section 6

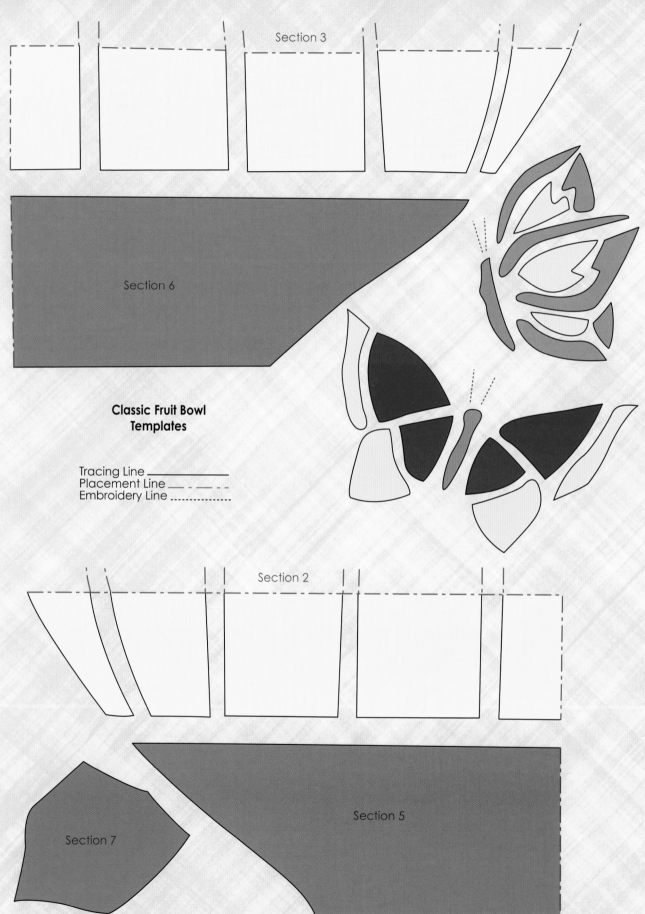

Section 3

Section 6

**Classic Fruit Bowl
Templates**

Tracing Line _____
Placement Line _ _ . _ _ . _
Embroidery Line . . . .

Section 2

Section 7

Section 5

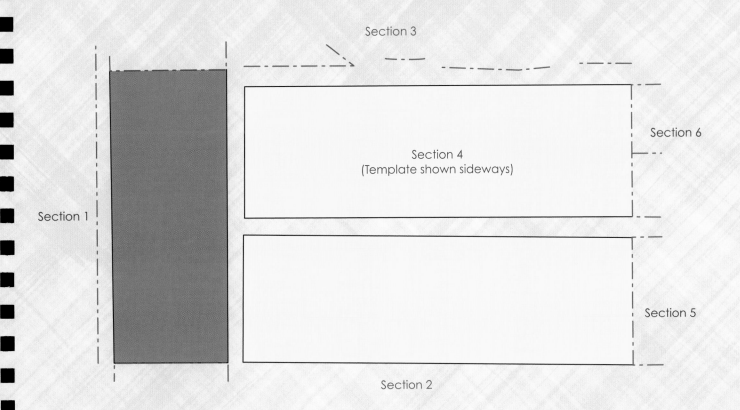

Section 3

Section 6

Section 1

Section 4
(Template shown sideways)

Section 5

Section 2

make it even easier

classic fruit bowl alternative

Finished Size: 28" x 22"

Fabric A (Background) -
  ¾ yard
  One 27½" x 21½" piece
Fabric B (Tiles) - ⅛ yard
Fabric C (Tile Accent) -
  ⅛ yard
  One ¼" x 42" strip
Appliqués - Assorted scraps
Backing - ¾ yard
Batting - 32" x 26"
Binding - ⅓ yard
  Three 2¾" x 42" strips
Steam-A-Seam 2® - 1½ yards

1. Refer to Adding the Appliqués on page 7, step 1, to prepare the pattern. Reverse individual element templates before tracing onto paper of fusible web. Place traced fruit and bowl on selected fabric scraps and cut out shapes. Place Steam-A-Seam 2® on wrong side of Fabric B and cut thirty-six 1⅜" squares, rounding corners.

2. Arrange all appliqués on Fabric A piece, trim tiles and tile accent to fit around bowl. Following manufacturer's instructions, fuse appliqués. Finish edges with machine satin stitch or decorative stitching if desired.

3. Referring to photo on page 6, and Embroidery Stitch Guide on page 110, use three strands of embroidery floss and Stem Stitch to add tendrils to fruit and antennae to butterflies.

4. Arrange and baste backing, batting, and top together, referring to page 110.

5. Hand or machine quilt as desired.

6. Sew 2¾" x 42" binding strips end-to-end to make one continuous 2¾"-wide binding strip. Refer to Binding the Quilt on page 111 and bind quilt to finish.

Don't sweat the small stuff! If the tiny mosaic pieces are intimidating, you can make the Classic Fruit Bowl using standard quick-fuse appliqué techniques. Just cut entire fruit appliqués and sew away!

le chanticleer
wall banner

Finished size: 20" x 38"

You'll always have something to crow about when this charming banner graces your wall.
Sunflowers and embellishments are stenciled on the fabric then highlighted with quilting
to make this banner simple and sensational. Quick-sew embellishments such as
buttons, beads, tabs, and a tassel add instant appeal.

fabric requirements & cutting instructions

Read all instructions before beginning and use ¼"-wide seam allowances throughout. Read Cutting the Strips and Pieces on page 108 prior to cutting fabrics.

Le Chanticleer Wall Banner 20" x 38"	FIRST CUT		SECOND CUT	
	Number of Strips or Pieces	Dimensions	Number of Pieces	Dimensions
Fabric A Background ⅝ yard	1 2	16" x 42" 1½" x 42"	1 1	16" x 12½" 16" x 6½"
Fabric B Block Background ⅜ yard	1	10½" square		
Fabric C Block Accent ⅛ yard	3	1" x 42"	2 2 2	1" x 16" 1" x 11½" 1" x 10½"
Fabric D Corner Setting Triangles ⅓ yard	1	8¾" x 42"	2	8¾" squares*
Fabric E Outside Border and Tabs ⅓ yard	3 3	5½" x 2" 1½" x 42"		

Appliqués - Assorted scraps
Backing - ⅔ yard
Batting - 24" x 42"
Buttons - Five 1"
Beads - Sixteen ³⁄₁₆" beads
Tassel
Mylar or Stencil Plastic
Craft Knife
Acrylic Paint -White, golden yellow, black & medium green
Fabric Medium
Palette Paper
¼" Stencil Brushes - four
Paper Towels

Stencil designs on two opposite corners of each square prior to cutting diagonally.

le chanticleer wall banner
finished size: 20" x 38"
photo: opposite page

getting started

This charming quilt consists of an appliquéd rooster, stenciled sunflower, and flourishes on a simple banner. Beads, buttons, tabs, and a tassel embellish the banner. Stenciling was completed prior to constructing the quilt. Refer to Accurate Seam Allowance on page 108 before making quilt. Press seams in direction of arrows.

stenciling fabric

Stenciling should be completed prior to construction of the quilt.

1. Refer to stencil patterns on page 18 and trace patterns onto Mylar. Cut design into mylar using a craft knife.

2. Place a small amount of paint on palette paper and add a few drops of fabric medium, following manufacturer's instructions.

3. The sunflower petals need to have a white undercoat applied prior to the yellow paint. Center petal stencil on 16" x 6½" Fabric A piece. Using a dry stencil brush, apply white paint to brush, tap off excess paint onto paper towel. If too much paint remains on brush, seepage can occur under stencil. It is very important to start with a dry brush; if any water is in brush, paint will run uncontrollably. Let brush rest on surface of fabric and swirl in a circular motion to apply white paint to sunflower petal area. Allow to dry completely. Repeat process for second sunflower on 16" x 12½" Fabric A piece. Clean brush after applying each color as dried paint will ruin brush.

4. Using new, dry stencil brush, apply golden yellow paint over white undercoat using the same method described in step 3. Allow to dry. Repeat for second sunflower.

5. Using dry stencil brush, black paint, and circle stencil, paint center of sunflower. Repeat for second sunflower.

6. Refer to photo and layout on pages 14 and 15, to arrange flourish stencil on Fabric A. Using a circular motion and the dry brush technique, stencil fabric with black paint.

7. Draw diagonal line on each 8¾" Fabric D square. Place flourish stencil on fabric with points 1¼" from drawn line, centering design left to right. Using dry stencil brush and medium green paint, stencil flourishes onto opposite corners of each square as shown.

8. After paint is completely dry, heat-set with hot iron and pressing cloth. Cut Fabric D squares on drawn lines.

making the quilt

1. Sew 10½" Fabric B square between two 1" x 10½" Fabric C pieces. Press toward Fabric B. Sew unit between two 1" x 11½" Fabric C pieces. Press.

2. Sew unit from step 1 between two Fabric D corner setting triangles as shown.

3. Sew two Fabric D corner setting triangles to remaining sides of unit from step 2 as shown. Press.

4. Sew 1" x 16" Fabric C strips to top and bottom of unit. Press toward strips.

5. Sew 16" x 6½" Fabric A piece to top of unit. Press.

6. Sew 16" x 12½" Fabric A piece to bottom of unit. Press. Measure and mark bottom of lower Fabric A section at center and 2¼" from Fabric C strip as shown. Align cutting guide at marks and cut off corner. Repeat for second corner.

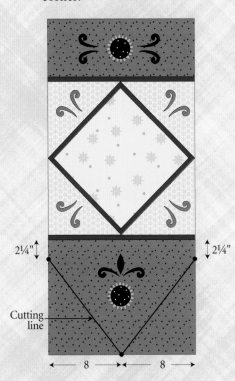

appliquéing the quilt

The instructions given are for quick-fuse appliqué. If hand appliqué is preferred, be sure to reverse all appliqué templates and add ¼"-wide seam allowances when cutting appliqué pieces. Refer to Hand Appliqué on page 109.

1. Referring to Quick-Fuse Appliqué on page 109, trace appliqué templates on page 19 for rooster.

2. Referring to photo and layout on pages 14 and 15, position and fuse appliqués on center square. Finish with machine satin stitch or decorative stitching as desired.

borders

1. Refer to photo and layout on pages 14 and 15. Sew 1½" x 42" Fabric A strips to sides of unit. Press seams toward Fabric A. Align ruler along lower edge of quilt and trim strip even with edge of quilt.

2. Sew 1½" x 42" Fabric E strips together end-to-end to make one continuous 1½"-wide strip. Measure through center of quilt from side-to-side and cut one 1½"-wide strip to this length. Sew to top of quilt. Press toward Fabric E.

3. Sew 1½"-wide strip to side of quilt. Press. Trim end of strip even with lower outer edge as shown. Repeat for remaining side.

4. Sew 1½"-wide strip to lower right edge of quilt. Press seam toward border. Trim ends of strip even with edges of quilt. Sew strip to lower left edge of quilt, including borders previously sewn. Press and trim. Repeat to sew lower right edge.

5. Fold 5½" x 2" Fabric E piece lengthwise with right sides together. Stitch along 5½" edges. Center seam along back and press seam allowance open. Turn right side out and press. Make three.

6. Fold tabs in half crosswise. Referring to photo and layout on pages 14 and 15, arrange tabs at top of quilt front, aligning raw edges. Pin or baste in place.

layering & finishing

1. Layer quilt top and backing, right sides together, on batting. Pin or baste around edges of quilt.

2. Using a ¼"-wide seam, sew around edges leaving a 5" opening for turning. Trim batting close to stitching. Trim backing ¼" from seam line. Clip corners and turn right side out. Press. Hand-stitch opening closed.

3. Baste, then machine or hand quilt as desired. We top-stitched close to outside edges, taking care to keep backing from showing on front.

4. Refer to photo and layout on pages 14 and 15 to position and sew beads for rooster eye and sunflower spots, buttons, and tassel to quilt.

**Le Chanticleer
Stencil Patterns**

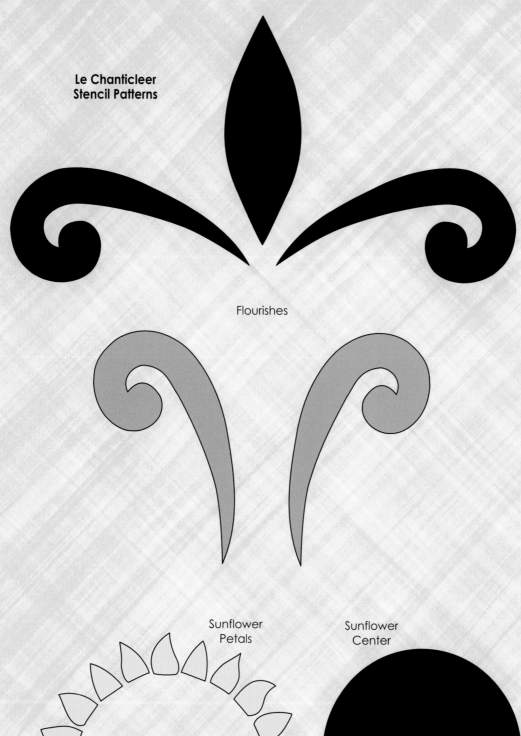

Flourishes

Sunflower
Petals

Sunflower
Center

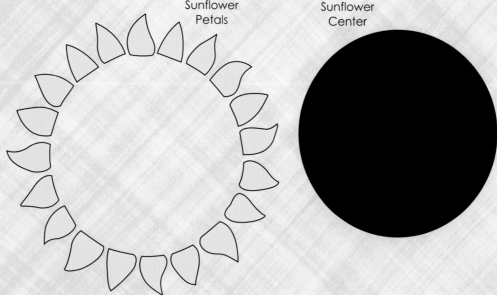

**Le Chanticleer
Quick Fuse Appliqué Template**

*Templates are reversed for use
with Quick-Fuse Appliqué
(page 109)*

Tracing Line _____
Tracing Line - - - - - - - - - - -
(will be hidden behind other fabrics)

fruit du jour
table quilt

Finished size: 43" square
Lattice ribbons intertwine showcasing luscious fruit on this classic table quilt.
Strip piecing and quick corner triangles make this quilt easy to piece. Fruit details
can be machine embroidered or appliquéd. Pick your preference!

fabric requirements & cutting instructions

Read all instructions before beginning and use ¼"-wide seam allowances throughout. Read Cutting the Strips and Pieces on page 108 prior to cutting fabrics.

Fruit du Jour Table Quilt 43" square	FIRST CUT		SECOND CUT	
	Number of Strips or Pieces	Dimensions	Number of Pieces	Dimensions
Fabric A Background ¾ yard	1	10" x 42"	4	10" squares*
	5	2½" x 42"	32	2½" squares
Fabric B Lattice and First Border ⅝ yard	2	3½" x 42"	16	3½" squares
	7	1½" x 42"		
BORDERS				
Second Border ¼ yard	4	1½" x 42"		
Third Border ½ yard	4	3½" x 42"		
Outside Border ⅝ yard	4	4½" x 42"		
Binding ½ yard	5	2¾" x 42"		

Backing - 2¾ yards
Batting - 49" x 49"
Stabilizer

*These pieces will be used for embroidery, then cut into four 6½" squares.

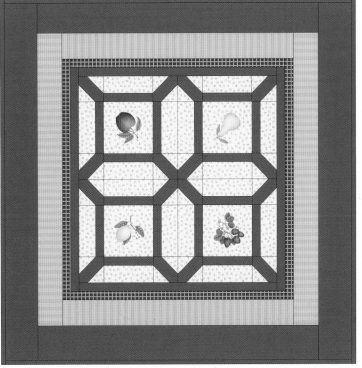

fruit du jour table quilt
finished size: 43" square
photo: opposite page

getting started

You will be making four blocks with embroidered centers. Blocks measure 12½" square unfinished.

Refer to Accurate Seam Allowance on page 108. Use the Assembly Line Method on page 108 whenever possible. Press seams in direction of arrows.

making the blocks

1. *The Good Life by Debbie Mumm®* embroidery card and a Bernina® artista 200E were used for this project. Refer to manufacturer's machine-embroidery guide to fasten fabric and stabilizer in hoop. Place 10" Fabric A square diagonally in embroidery hoop to embroider design on point. Refer to photo and layout on pages 20 and 21 and stitch design. Remove stabilizer and trim fabric to 6½" square. Make four.

2. Sew 2½" x 42" Fabric A strip to 1½" x 42" Fabric B strip. Press. Make three.

42
2½
1½

Make 3

3. From strip sets, cut sixteen 6½"-wide segments.

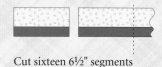

Cut sixteen 6½" segments

4. Sew 6½" Fabric A square from step 1 between two units from step 3 as shown. Press. Make four.

6½

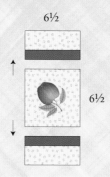

6½

Make 4

5. Refer to Quick Corner Triangles on page 108. Sew two 2½" Fabric A squares to 3½" Fabric B square as shown. Press. Make sixteen.

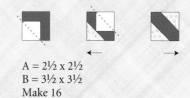

A = 2½ x 2½
B = 3½ x 3½
Make 16

6. Sew unit from step 3 between two units from step 5 as shown. Press. Make eight.

Make 8

7. Sew unit from step 4 between two units from step 6 as shown. Press. Make four.

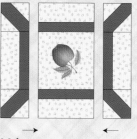

Make 4
Block measures 12½" square

tip — appliqué alternatives

If desired, appliqués and hand embroidery may be used in place of machine embroidery. Add appliqués just prior to Layering and Finishing. Refer to Appliqué Templates on pages 24-25, and Quick-Fuse Appliqué on page 109. Trace, arrange, and fuse appliqués to center of blocks. Finish appliqués with machine satin stitch or decorative stitching as desired.

If hand appliqué is preferred, refer to Hand Appliqué on page 109.

Refer to Embroidery Guide on page 110. Use two strands of embroidery floss and a Satin or Stem Stitch for stems, a Stem Stitch for leaf veins, and French Knots for blossom centers.

borders

1. Referring to Adding the Borders on page 110, measure quilt through center from side to side. Cut two 1½"-wide Fabric B strips to that measurement. Sew to top and bottom of quilt. Press seams toward border.

2. Measure quilt through center from top to bottom including the borders just added. Cut two 1½"-wide Fabric B strips to that measurement. Sew to sides of quilt. Press toward border.

3. Repeat steps 1 and 2 to measure, trim, and sew 1½"-wide Second Border and 3½"-wide Third Border strips to quilt. Press seams toward borders.

4. Sew 4½" x 42" Outside Border strips end-to-end to make one continuous 4½"-wide strip. Refer to steps 1 and 2 to measure, trim, and sew 4½"-wide Outside Border to quilt. Press.

embroidery card source information

The Good Life by Debbie Mumm® embroidery card features fruit and flower motifs. It is available from a Bernina® dealer or online at www.embroideryonline.com.

fresh fruit chair covers

(for one chair cover)

Fabric A (Center Square) - ½ yard
  One 12" square
Fabric B (First Border) - ⅙ yard
  Two 2" x 14" strips
  Two 2" x 12" strips
Fabric C (Corner Setting Triangles and Outside Border) - approximately ⅞ yard*
  Two 11" squares, cut once diagonally
  Two 5" x 27" strips
  Two 5" x 19" strips
Batting - ⅝ yard or more
Stabilizer
Tacks or staples

* Our chair cover is wrapped around an 18" square wood base with added padding. If your chair cushion is larger, make adjustments in the width and length of 5"-wide Fabric C strips. Use ½"-wide seams throughout.

finished size: 18" square

Squares on point spotlight a favorite piece of fruit on these easy and appealing chair cushion covers.

making the chair cover

1. The designs on this project were made with *The Good Life by Debbie Mumm*® embroidery card by Bernina® and a Bernina artista 200E. Place 12" Fabric A square and stabilizer diagonally in embroidery hoop to embroider design on point, referring to machine embroidery guide. Stitch design and remove stabilizer, if desired.

2. Using **½"-wide seams** throughout, refer to photo to sew 12" embroidered Fabric A square between two 2" x 12" Fabric B strips. Press. Sew unit between two 2" x 14" Fabric B strips. Press.

3. Referring to photo, sew unit from step 2 between two Fabric C Corner Setting Triangles. Fabric C triangles will extend slightly past Fabric B edges. Press. Sew unit between remaining two Fabric C triangles. Press.

4. Sew unit from step 3 between two 5" x 19" Fabric C strips. Press. Sew this unit between two 5" x 27" Fabric C strips. Press.

5. Remove cushion base from chair. Wrap batting around cushion base. Cover with chair cover. Fasten chair cover edges to bottom of base with tacks or staples. Attach chair cushion to chair.

companion project

classic fruit bowl pillow

A pillow panel from Debbie Mumm's® Classic Fruit Bowl Fabric Collection was used to make this simple pillow. Three different fruit bowl designs are available as pillow panels in this fabric line.

finished size: 13½" x 14½"

This beautiful fruit bowl pillow looks like a complicated sewing project, but it is super simple–a preprinted panel makes this project very quick and easy!

making the pillow

1. Cut out pillow panel including two rows of surrounding checks, adding ¼" seam allowance on all sides.

2. Layer lining, batting, and pillow panel and baste.

3. Hand or machine quilt pillow top as desired. Outline quilting was used for the fruit, bowl, and tiles to add dimension. Stipple quilting in the red background area makes the fruit bowl "pop."

4. Refer to Finishing Pillows on page 111 to sew backing pieces to pillow and make pillow form.

   Pillow panels can also be used to make chair cushions, placemats, table runners, or as the center of quilt blocks.

layering & finishing

1. Cut backing fabric in half crosswise. Sew pieces together to make one 80" x 49" (approximate) backing piece. Press. Trim backing to 49" square. Arrange and baste backing, batting, and top together, referring to Layering the Quilt on page 110.

2. Hand or machine quilt as desired.

3. Sew 2¾" x 42" binding strips end-to-end to make one continuous 2¾"-wide strip. Refer to Binding the Quilt on page 111 and bind quilt to finish.

Strawberries & Blossoms

Tracing Line _____
Tracing Line - - - - - - - - - - - -
(will be hidden behind other fabrics)
Embroidery Line · · · · · · · · · · · · · · · · ·

**Fruit du Jour
Quick-Fuse Appliqué Templates**

*Templates are reversed for use
with Quick-Fuse Appliqué
(page109)*

Luscious Lemon

Perfect Pear

Delicious Apple

leaf garland
french bucket

A garland of simple leaves adds decorative charm to this easy painting project.
Fill the French bucket with a beautiful bouquet of flowers for a striking centerpiece.

Leaf Garland French Bucket

MATERIALS NEEDED

Galvanized tin French bucket - available at craft stores

Vinegar

Acrylic paints in medium red, dark red, ivory, light green, medium green, medium gold, and dark gold

Assorted paint brushes

Sea sponge

Antiquing medium

Two-step crackle medium

Matte spray varnish

Tracing paper

Graphite transfer paper

Pencil

Laurel Leaf Template

painting the french bucket

Allow each new paint application to dry thoroughly before moving to the next step. Refer to photo with each step. Read all instructions before beginning.

1. Wash galvanized bucket with vinegar to remove oils. Rinse well and allow to dry.

2. Determine placement of each paint color using the details of your French bucket as a guide.

3. Paint bottom section of bucket medium red and allow to dry.

4. Place small amounts of medium red and dark red paints on a palette or paper plate. Dip sea sponge in water, wring thoroughly, then dip in medium red and dark red paints. Blot several times on palette. Using a tapping motion, sponge color onto the medium red basecoat, using a light touch for a stippled effect. Stipple entire red area.

5. Paint center band ivory. Trace Laurel Leaf template onto tracing paper. Use graphite transfer paper to transfer laurel leaves onto ivory band, spacing evenly, and centering in the ivory band. Paint leaves medium green. When dry, use a fine paintbrush to add veins with light green paint.

6. Paint top section of bucket medium gold. When dry, use a ½"-wide paintbrush to paint dark gold stripes on medium gold band.

7. Paint raised areas to highlight. Use gold paint to highlight raised band between the red and ivory sections and use dark red to highlight raised band between the ivory and gold sections. Paint top and bottom rims and handles medium green.

8. When painting is complete, apply Step One of crackle medium over ivory/leaf area. Allow to dry as specified by manufacturer, then apply Step Two. This will form crackles in the finish of Step One.

9. Spray bucket with matte varnish and allow to dry.

10. Following manufacturer's directions, apply antiquing medium over entire can, wiping off as desired for an antique finish. Antiquing will make the crackles on the ivory band more prominent. Allow to dry.

11. Spray completed bucket with matte varnish.

french country

curtains

Red fabric ribbons add gentle sway to these simple curtains dressed up with embroidered strawberries, lemons, and a pear. To make them even easier, use a fruit-print fabric or a border print instead of embroidery.

fabric requirements & cutting instructions

Read all instructions before beginning and use ½"-wide seams throughout.

French Country Curtains	WIDTH	LENGTH	YOUR MEASUREMENT
Fabric A Curtain Background	1.25 times width of window	Half of window length minus 7"	
Fabric B Border	Same as Fabric A	9"	
Fabric C Ties	5"	2 times length of curtain	
Lining	Width of curtain plus 1"	Length of curtain plus 1"	
Rod Pocket	Finished width of curtain	5"	
Two 1" Buttons			

(Reverse Embroidery/Appliqué on left side of curtain)

getting started

Measure your window for a custom fit curtain. Add embroidery or appliqué to personalize the design. A wide border and ties add accents. **Use ½"-wide seams throughout.**

making the curtain

1. Measure width and length of window and use Fabric Chart above to determine amount of fabric needed for curtain. If piecing the curtain is necessary, be sure to include ½" seam allowance for each piece of fabric.

2. Cut Fabric A curtain background to achieve correct width. Stitch pieces together, if necessary.

3. If not embroidering, skip to step 6. Embroidered designs are from *The Good Life by Debbie Mumm®* Embroidery Card by Bernina® (see page 23). The curtain was embroidered in three sections using a mega hoop and the Bernina® artista 200E. Some images were reversed. For the lemon, all flowers and one leaf were eliminated. To determine embroidery placement, make a paper copy of machine embroidery templates for each embroidered design. Mark lengthwise center of Background fabric. Position paper copies to determine desired placement of designs. Use a temporary fabric marker to make a small "+" on Background fabric where center of each design should be stitched.

tip *If hand or machine appliqué is desired, refer to Hand Appliqué or Quick-Fuse Appliqué on page 109, and Fruit Appliqué Templates on pages 24, 25, and 31. For hand appliqué, reverse templates as needed and add ¼"-wide seam allowance. Add appliqués to curtain after step 6, before sewing the lining.*

4. With a matching or lighter color thread than Fabric A, baste a line parallel to bottom of curtain and through center of each "+".

5. For machine embroidery, place fabric and stabilizer in hoop according to embroidery machine instructions. Center embroidery hoop and hoop template over each "+". Basting thread should line up with hoop template or be parallel to it. Remove template and basting thread just prior to stitching embroidery, then stitch embroidery designs.

6. If using more than one 9" x 42" Border strip, sew strips together end-to-end to make one continuous 9"-wide strip. With right sides together, sew border to bottom of background fabric. Press seam allowance toward border.

7. Pin curtain and lining, right sides together. Using a ½"-wide seam sew around all edges leaving a 6"-wide opening for turning. Clip corners, turn right side out, and press. Hand-stitch opening closed.

8. Press short ends of Rod Pocket fabric under ¼" and ¼" again. Stitch along folded inside edge. Press under lengthwise edges of Rod Pocket fabric ½". Pin wrong side of pocket to right side of lining at top of curtain. Stitch top and bottom of pocket to lining and curtain through all layers as shown. Hang curtain on rod.

9. Fold Fabric C in half lengthwise, right sides together, and stitch along the length. Center seam along back and press seam allowance open. Turn right side out and press. Make sure seam is in center of tie. Make two. Turn ¼" of raw edges to inside and hand or machine stitch closed.

10. Hang ties lengthwise over both sides of curtain. Adjust ties. Overlap ends of tie to determine drape of curtain. Mark amount of overlap with pin and remove ties. Trim end of ties if necessary.

11. Sew a buttonhole and button on each tie as shown, positioning button for overlap. Fasten ties on curtain then adjust drape and fullness as desired.

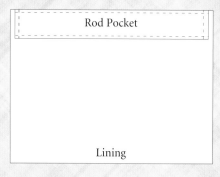

Rod Pocket

Lining

tip decorating tip

The red plaid wallpaper featured in the French Country kitchen is from the Debbie Mumm Home Collection™ by Imperial. Visit www.ihdg.com or your local wallpaper store.

French Country Curtains
Quick Fuse Appliqué Templates
- -
*Templates are reversed for use
with Quick-Fuse Appliqué
(page 109)*

Tracing Line _____
Tracing Line _ _ _ _ _ _ _ _ _ _ _ _ _
(will be hidden behind other fabrics)
Embroidery Line _ _ _ _ _ _ _ _ _ _

make it even easier

appliqué alternatives

In place of embroidery use an appliqué technique.

For quick-fuse appliqué refer to directions for Quick-Fuse Appliqué on page 109 before cutting selected fruit motifs.

For hand appliqué cut out fruit motifs adding ¼"-wide seam allowances and refer to directions for Hand Appliqué on page 109.

Or try a *broderie perse* technique. Cut out fruit motifs from a printed fabric and appliqué as desired.

Small Strawberry Bunch

new country traditions

Create new family traditions in a room filled with the bold colors and architectural designs of these sophisticated country-style quilts. From the framed art ensemble above the mantel, to the striking fireplace screen, to the intricate interplay of colors on the lap quilt, you'll find your own unique style with these elegant quilts.

quilted wall art
ensemble

Framing and dimensional embellishments give this quilt grouping above the mantel great decorating style! Neutral colors highlighted with vivid black give these easily-pieced quilts an architectural flair. Embellished with a pieced "pillow," buttons, and beads, this grouping will be the focal point of your living room.

fabric requirements & cutting instructions

Read all instructions before beginning and use ¼"-wide seam allowances throughout. Read Cutting the Strips and Pieces on page 108 prior to cutting fabrics.

quilted wall art ensemble
(shown unembellished)
photo: opposite page

Large Wall Art Quilt 27" x 27" (Framed)	FIRST CUT		SECOND CUT	
	Number of Strips or Pieces	Dimensions	Number of Pieces	Dimensions
Fabric A Background ¼ yard	1	5½" x 42"	4	5½" squares
			4	3½" squares
Fabric B Accent Border and First Border ⅓ yard	1	5½" x 42"	4	5½" squares
			4	2½" x 4½"
	2	1¼" x 42"	4	1¼" x 6¼"
			4	1¼" x 5½"
Fabric C Light Cheverons ⅛ yard	1	2½" x 42"	16	2½" squares
Fabric D Dark Cheveron ¼ yard	1	5½" x 42"	8	5½" x 2½"
Fabric E Center Star Points ⅛ yard	1	2½" x 42"	8	2½" squares
Fabric F Center Square Scrap	1	4½" square		
Fabric G Four-Patch Assorted scraps in four fabrics	1	5½" square		
	1*	3" square		
	Cut for each of four fabrics			
BORDERS				
Second Border ⅙ yard	2	1¾" x 42"	4	1¾" x 7½"
			4	1¾" x 6¼"
Outside Border ½ yard	3	4½" x 42"		
Backing - ⅞ yard Batting - 28" x 28" Polyester Fiberfill Assorted Buttons and Beads				

Small Wall Art Quilts(makes 2) 11½" x 16½" (Framed)	FIRST CUT		SECOND CUT	
	Number of Strips or Pieces	Dimensions	Number of Pieces	Dimensions
Fabric A Background ⅛ yard	1	2½" x 42"	8	2½" squares
Fabric B Light Cheveron ⅛ yard	1	2½" x 42"	16	2½" squares
Fabric C Dark Cheveron ⅛ yard	1	2½" x 42"	4	2½" x 5½"
BORDERS				
First Border ⅛ yard	2	1" x 42"	4	1" x 10½"
			4	1" x 4½"
Second Border ⅛ yard	2	1¼" x 42"	4	1¼" x 12"
			4	1¼" x 5½"
Outside Border ⅓ yard	3	3" x 42"	4	3" x 17"
			4	3" x 7"
Backing - ⅜ yard Batting - two 13" x 18" pieces Assorted Buttons and Beads				

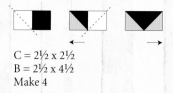

getting started

Instructions are for one Large Wall Art Quilt and two Small Wall Art Quilts. Refer to Accurate Seam Allowance on page 108. Use the Assembly Line Method on page 108 whenever possible. Press seams in direction of arrows.

making the large wall art quilt

1. Refer to Quick Corner Triangles on page 108. Sew 5½" Fabric A square to 5½" Fabric B square as shown. Press. Make four.

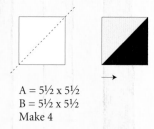

A = 5½ x 5½
B = 5½ x 5½
Make 4

2. Sew 3½" Fabric A square to unit from step 1 as shown. Press. Make four.

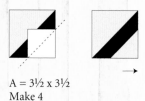

A = 3½ x 3½
Make 4

3. Sew 1¼" x 5½" Fabric B piece to unit from step 2 as shown. Press. Make four. Sew 1¼" x 6¼" Fabric B piece to unit as shown. Press. Make four.

5½

1¼

Make 4

1¼

6¼

Make 4

4. Sew 1¾" x 6¼" Second Border piece to unit from step 3, as shown. Press. Make four, two of each variation.

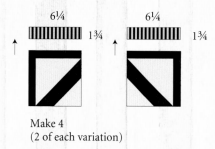

6¼   1¾   6¼   1¾

Make 4
(2 of each variation)

5. Sew 1¾" x 7½" Second Border piece to unit from step 4, as shown. Press. Make four, two of each variation.

1¾   1¾

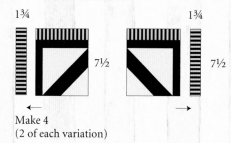

7½   7½

Make 4
(2 of each variation)

6. Making quick corner triangle units, sew two 2½" Fabric C squares to 2½" x 4½" Fabric B piece as shown. Press. Make four.

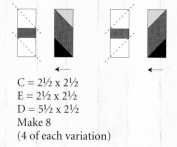

C = 2½ x 2½
B = 2½ x 4½
Make 4

7. Making quick corner triangle units, sew 2½" Fabric C and 2½" Fabric E squares to 5½" x 2½" Fabric D piece as shown. Press. Make eight, four of each variation.

C = 2½ x 2½
E = 2½ x 2½
D = 5½ x 2½
Make 8
(4 of each variation)

8. Sew units from step 7 together in pairs, as shown. Press seams open. Make four.

Make 4

9. Sew unit from step 6 to unit from step 8 as shown. Press. Make four.

Make 4

10. Sew unit from step 9 between two units from step 5 as shown. Press. Make two.

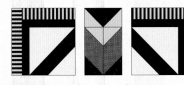

Make 2

11. Sew 4½" Fabric F square between two units from step 9 as shown. Press.

4½

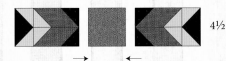

4½

12. Sew unit from step 11 between two units from step 10 as shown. Press. Block measures 18½" square.

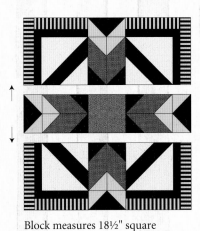

Block measures 18½" square

framed finish

One 27" square frame (outside dimension lumber width 2½" finished)
Two 11½" x 16½" frames (outside dimension lumber width 1½" finished)
Sandpaper
Acrylic paint in dark red and black
Matte spray varnish
Dark brown antiquing medium
Assorted paintbrushes
Old toothbrush
Acid-free mat board
Picture hangers

Add a fine art finish to wall quilts with painted frames. A few easy steps will provide just the right color and finish to showcase your quilts.

painting the frames

1. Sand frames to remove any gloss or oils. Use tack cloth or damp rag to remove residue.

2. Basecoat frames with dark red paint. Allow to dry. A second coat may be necessary for complete coverage.

3. Distress frames by sanding edges with sandpaper until wood shows through.

4. Spray with matte varnish. Allow to dry.

5. Mix small amount of water with black paint and fill an old toothbrush with mixture. Rub thumb over bristles to add black paint spatters. Practice technique on a piece of paper before trying it on frames. If spatters are too heavy or large, use cotton swab to remove unwanted spatters before paint dries. Allow to dry.

6. Following manufacturer's directions, apply antiquing medium to frames. Use a rag to rub off antiquing until desired look is achieved. Allow to dry.

7. Spray frames with matte varnish.

8. From back of frame, measure maximum opening including rabbet (groove on back side of frame). Subtract ⅛" from both measurements and cut mat board to that measurement. If frames do not have rabbets, cut mat board at least ¼" larger than inside dimensions on all sides. Wrap quilt pieces around mat boards and secure as desired. Attach to frames as desired.

9. Add your choice of hanger and install on wall.

border for the large wall art quilt

1. Referring to Adding the Borders on page 110, measure quilt through center from side to side. From one 4½"-wide Outside Border strip, cut two pieces to that measurement. Sew to top and bottom of quilt. Press seams toward border.

2. Measure quilt through center from top to bottom including the borders just added. Cut two 4½"-wide Outside Border strips to that measurement. Sew to sides of quilt. Press.

layering & quilting

1. Arrange and baste backing, batting, and top together, referring to Layering the Quilt on page 110.

2. Hand or machine quilt as desired.

adding the four-patch pillow

1. Referring to photo on page 34, sew two 3" Fabric G squares together. Press. Make two. Sew units together as shown. Press.

2. Place unit from step 1 and 5½" Fabric G square right sides together. Stitch around edges using a ¼"-wide seam and leaving a 2" opening for turning. Clip corners, turn right side out, and press.

3. Stuff pillow to desired fullness with polyester fiberfill. Hand-stitch opening closed.

4. Select buttons in graduated sizes and with interesting edge treatments. Stack buttons with a bead on top and sew through pillow center, pulling tightly. Sew a bead to each corner of pillow.

5. Referring to photo on page 34, tack pillow on point to center of quilt. Sew buttons to quilt, one under each bead at pillow corners to accent beads.

6. Refer to Framed Finish on page 37 to paint frame and install quilt, or to Make It Even Easier on page 39 to bind quilt.

making the small wall art quilts

1. Refer to Quick Corner Triangles on page 108. Sew one 2½" Fabric A square to one 2½" Fabric B square as shown. Make eight. Press four seams toward Fabric A and four toward Fabric B.

A = 2½ x 2½
B = 2½ x 2½
Make 8

2. Making quick corner triangle units, sew two 2½" Fabric B squares to 2½" x 5½" Fabric C piece. Press. Make four, two of each variation.

B = 2½ x 2½
C = 2½ x 5½
Make 4
(2 of each variation)

3. Sew unit from step 2 between two units from step 1 as shown. Press. Make four, two of each variation.

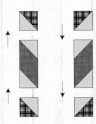

Make 4
(2 of each variation)

4. Sew units from step 3 together in pairs, as shown. Press. Make two.

Make 2

borders

1. Sew 1" x 4½" First Border pieces to top and bottom of quilt. Press toward borders. Sew 1" x 10½" First Border pieces to sides of quilt. Press toward borders. Make two.

2. Repeat step 1 to sew 1¼" x 5½" and 1¼" x 12" Second Border pieces, then 3" x 7" and 3" x 17 Outside Border pieces to quilt. Press toward borders. Make two.

layering & quilting

1. Arrange and baste backing, batting, and top together, referring to Layering the Quilt on page 110.

2. Hand or machine quilt as desired.

3. Select buttons in graduated sizes and with interesting edge treatments. Stack buttons with a bead on top and sew to top portion of each quilt, referring to photo below for placement.

4. Stack beads on top of button and sew to cheveron point of each quilt as shown. Sew two oblong and two round beads at bottom of button.

5. Refer to Framed Finish on page 37 to paint frame and to install quilt, or to Make It Even Easier, below, to bind quilt.

make it even easier ez

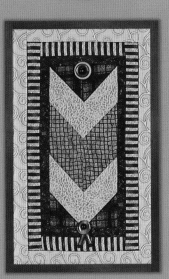

If painting isn't your expertise, simply add binding to finish your quilts.

wall art ensemble with binding

large wall art quilt

Finished size: 23" x 23"
　Outside Border - ⅓ yard
　　Two 2½" x 18½" strips
　　Two 2½" x 22½" strips
　Binding - ⅓ yard
　　Three 2¾" x 42" strips

small wall art quilts

Finished size: 9½" x 14½"
　(Makes two)
　Outside Border - ⅛ yard
　　Four 1½" x 7" pieces
　　Four 1½" x 14" pieces
　Binding - ⅓ yard
　　Three 2¾" x 42" strips

binding the quilts

1. Refer to Quilted Wall Art Ensemble instructions, pages 36-39, substituting Outside Border yardage and fabric cuts with those listed at left.

2. Refer to Binding the Quilt on page 111. Measure quilt through center from side to side. Cut two 2¾"-wide strips to this measurement. Sew to top and bottom of quilt. Press seam toward binding.

3. Measure quilt through center from top to bottom including the binding just added. Cut two 2¾"-wide binding strips to this measurement. Sew to sides of quilt. Press.

4. Fold binding to back of quilt and hand-stitch in place.

rising star
fireplace screen

Finished size: 35" x 35"

Warm up your fireplace when it's not in use by constructing a dramatic, yet simple, fireplace screen.
Quick corner triangles make this quilt easy, and the frame is made from a twin bed frame found at a
thrift shop. This quilt would also make a striking wall quilt, or construct four star blocks for a lap quilt.

fabric requirements & cutting instructions

Read all instructions before beginning and use ¼"-wide seam allowances throughout. Read Cutting the Strips and Pieces on page 108 prior to cutting fabrics.

Rising Star Fireplace Screen Quilt 35" x 35"	FIRST CUT		SECOND CUT	
	Number of Strips or Pieces	Dimensions	Number of Pieces	Dimensions
Fabric A Center Square & Background ⅝ yard	1	7½" x 42"	4	7½" squares
			1	5½" square
	1	4½" x 42"	8	4½" x 5"
	1	3" x 42"	8	3" squares
	1	2½" x 42"	8	2½" squares
Fabric B Center Square Triangles, Star Border, & First Border ⅝ yard	2	3" x 42"	8	3" x 5"
			4	3" squares
	3	2½" x 42"	8	2½" x 5½"
			20	2½" squares
	4	1½" x 42"		
Fabric C Star Border Accent ⅓ yard	3	2½" x 42"	8	2½" x 5"
			20	2½" squares
Fabric D Star Points ⅓ yard	2	5" x 42"	8	5" x 5½"
Fabric E Center Square Border ⅛ yard	1	2" x 42"	2	2" x 8½"
			2	2" x 5½"
Fabric F Center Square Second Border & Outside Border* ½ yard	1	1" x 42"	2	1" x 9½"
			2	1" x 8½"
	4	3" x 42"		
Binding ⅜ yard	4	2¾" x 42"		

Backing - 1⅛ yards
Batting - 40" x 40"

*Outside border size may need to be adjusted to accommodate framework.

rising star fireplace screen quilt
finished size: 35" x 35"
photo: opposite page

getting started

Refer to Accurate Seam Allowance on page 108. Use the Assembly Line Method on page 108 whenever possible. Press seams in direction of arrows.

making the blocks

1. Refer to Quick Corner Triangles on page 108. Sew 2½" Fabric A square to 2½" Fabric B square as shown. Press. Make eight.

A = 2½ x 2½
B = 2½ x 2½
Make 8

2. Making quick corner triangle units, sew two 2½" Fabric C squares to 2½" x 5½" Fabric B piece as shown. Press. Make eight, four of each variation.

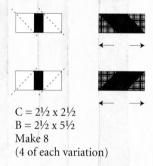

C = 2½ x 2½
B = 2½ x 5½
Make 8
(4 of each variation)

3. Sew unit from step 1 to unit from step 2 as shown. Press. Make eight, four of each variation.

Unit 1   Unit 2

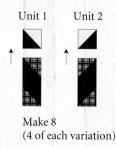

Make 8
(4 of each variation)

4. Sew 7½" Fabric A square to Unit 1 from step 3 as shown. Press. Make four.

7½

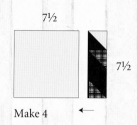

7½

Make 4 ←

5. Making quick corner triangle units, sew 2½" Fabric B square to 2½" Fabric C square as shown. Press. Make four.

B = 2½ x 2½
C = 2½ x 2½
Make 4

6. Sew Unit 2 from step 3 to unit from step 5 as shown. Press. Make four.

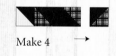

Make 4 →

7. Sew unit from step 4 to unit from step 6 as shown. Press. Make four.

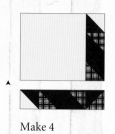

Make 4

8. Making quick corner triangle units, sew 2½" Fabric B square to 4½" x 5" Fabric A piece as shown. Press. Make eight, four of each variation.

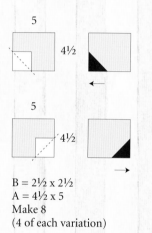

5

4½

5

4½

B = 2½ x 2½
A = 4½ x 5
Make 8
(4 of each variation)

9. Sew units from step 8 together in pairs as shown. Press. Make four.

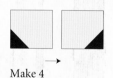

Make 4

10. Sew 2½" x 5" Fabric C piece to 3" x 5" Fabric B piece as shown. Press. Make eight.

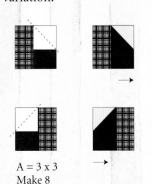

2½   3

5

→

Make 8

11. Making quick corner triangle units, sew 3" Fabric A square to unit from step 10 as shown. Press. Make eight, four of each variation.

A = 3 x 3
Make 8
(4 of each variation)

12. Making quick corner triangle units, position and sew unit from step 11 to 5" x 5½" Fabric D piece as shown. Press. Prior to stitching, flip back unit to see if positioning is correct. Make eight, four of each variation.

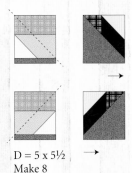

D = 5 x 5½   →
Make 8
(4 of each variation)

making the screen framework

Black acrylic paint
Assorted paintbrushes
Matte spray varnish
Dark brown antiquing medium
Sandpaper
Decorative posts and cross pieces*
Two metal shelf brackets
   (triangular shape)
Hook and loop tape

*Framework for screen shown is made from a twin bed headboard and footboard purchased at a thrift shop. The footboard was cut down and the two pieces were joined by drilling holes in the posts and using wooden dowels and wood glue to secure. The width of a twin headboard is the perfect size for this quilt. Check thrift shops and salvage stores for interesting furniture possibilities or architectural elements (like newel posts) to use for this project. If necessary, the quilt can be altered in size by adjusting or eliminating the outside border to fit a thrift shop "find."

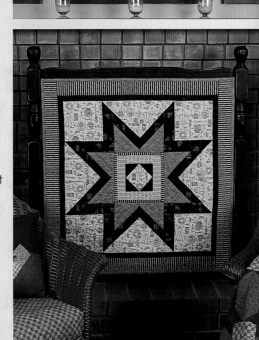

A simple framework adds classic character to the fireplace screen.

constructing the frame

1. Construct framework and sand or strip any existing finish, if necessary.

2. Paint entire piece with black acrylic paint. Allow to dry. A second coat may be necessary for good coverage.

3. Distress piece by sanding edges.

4. Spray with matte spray varnish. Allow to dry.

5. Apply dark brown antiquing medium to tone down distressed areas. Follow manufacturer's directions for best results.

6. Screw on metal shelf brackets at frame base to hold framework upright (see photo at right).

7. Determine where quilt will be placed. Sew hook and loop tape onto quilt in several appropriate places across the top and bottom.

8. Glue or place self-adhesive hook and loop tape onto framework at corresponding places and attach quilt.

13. Sew units from step 12 together in pairs as shown. Press. Make four.

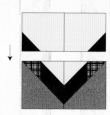

Make 4

14. Sew unit from step 9 to unit from step 13 as shown. Press. Make four.

Make 4

15. Sew unit from step 14 between two units from step 7 as shown. Press. Make two.

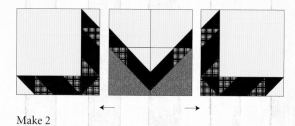

Make 2

16. Making quick corner triangles, sew two 3" Fabric B squares to opposite corners of 5½" Fabric A square as shown. Press. Repeat to sew two 3" Fabric B squares to remaining two corners. Press.

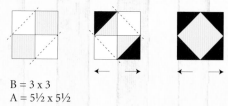

B = 3 x 3
A = 5½ x 5½

17. Sew unit from step 16 between two 2" x 5½" Fabric E pieces. Press toward Fabric E. Sew two 2" x 8½" Fabric E pieces to remaining sides. Press.

18. Sew two 1" x 8½" Fabric F pieces to top and bottom of unit from step 17. Press toward Fabric F. Sew 1" x 9½" Fabric F pieces to sides. Press.

19. Sew unit from step 18 between two units from step 14 as shown. Press.

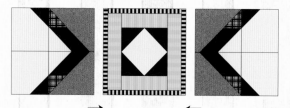

20. Referring to photo and layout on pages 40 and 41, sew unit from step 19 between two units from step 15. Press. Unit measures 27½" square.

borders

1. Refer to Adding the Borders on page 110. Measure quilt through center from side to side. Cut two 1½"-wide Fabric B strips to that measurement. Sew to top and bottom of quilt. Press seams toward border.

2. Measure quilt through center from top to bottom, including borders just added. Cut two 1½"-wide Fabric B strips to that measurement. Sew to sides of quilt. Press.

3. Refer to steps 1 and 2 to measure, trim, and sew 3" Fabric F strips to top, bottom, and sides of quilt. Press seams toward border.

layering & finishing

1. Arrange and baste backing, batting, and top together, referring to Layering the Quilt on page 110.

2. Hand or machine quilt as desired.

3. Sew 2¾" x 42" binding strips end-to-end to make one continuous 2¾"-wide strip. Refer to Binding the Quilt on page 111 and bind quilt to finish.

rising star lap quilt

finished size: 62" x 62"

Fabric A (Center Square & Background) - 2 yards
  Sixteen 7½" squares
  Four 5½" squares
  Thirty-two 4½" x 5" pieces
  Thirty-two 3" squares
  Thirty-two 2½" squares
Fabric B (Center Square Triangles, Star Border & First Border - 1⅝ yards
  Thirty-two 3" x 5" pieces
  Sixteen 3" squares
  Thirty-two 2½" x 5½" pieces
  Eighty 2½" squares
  Six 1½" x 42" strips
Fabric C (Star Border Accent) - ¾ yard
  Thirty-two 2½" x 5" pieces
  Eighty 2½" squares
Fabric D (Star Points) - ¾ yard
  Thirty-two 5" x 5½" pieces
Fabric E (Center Square Border) - ⅓ yard
  Eight 2" x 8½" pieces
  Eight 2" x 5½" pieces
Fabric F (Center Square Second Border & Outside Border) - ⅔ yard
  Six 3" x 42" strips
  Eight 1" x 9½" pieces
  Eight 1" x 8½" pieces
Binding - ⅝ yard
  Seven 2¾" x 42" strips
Backing - 4 yards
Batting - 70" x 70"

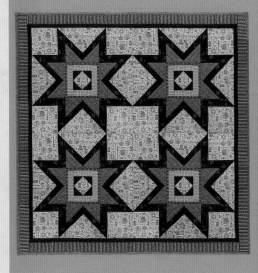

You'll be a star when you make this lap quilt for friends or family! Four Rising Star Blocks are joined to make this visually appealing quilt. Perfect to display on a wall or drape over a chair, this quilt will add dramatic color and style to your decorating scheme.

making the quilt

Read all instructions before beginning and use ¼"-wide seam allowances throughout. Refer to Accurate Seam Allowance and Assembly Line Method on page 108.

1. Refer to Rising Star Fireplace Screen Quilt, pages 42-44, steps 1 through 20. Repeat each step four times to make four 27½" square blocks.

2. Refer to photo to arrange and sew two rows with two blocks each. Press. Sew rows together. Press.

borders

1. Sew 1½" x 42"" Fabric B strips end-to-end to make one continuous 1½"-wide strip. Refer to Adding the Borders on page 110. Measure quilt through center from side to side. Cut two 1½"-wide strips to that measurement. Sew to top and bottom of quilt. Press seams toward border.

2. Measure quilt through center from top to bottom, including borders just added. Cut two 1½"-wide Fabric B strips to that measurement. Sew to sides of quilt. Press.

3. Refer to steps 1 and 2 to join, measure, trim, and sew 3"-wide Fabric F strips to top, bottom, and sides of quilt. Press seams toward border.

layering & finishing

1. Arrange and baste backing, batting, and top together, referring to Layering the Quilt on page 110.

2. Hand or machine quilt as desired.

3. Sew 2¾" x 42" binding strips end-to-end to make one continuous 2¾"-wide strip. Refer to Binding the Quilt on page 111 and bind quilt to finish.

country paths
lap quilt

Finished size: 60" x 72"

Add decorating pizzazz to sofa or chair with the sophisticated, yet traditional, look of this inviting lap quilt. Strong, rich colors play off each other in a pattern that looks complex, but is easy to piece. A repeating block makes it assembly-line-quick and a pieced sashing is another simplifying secret.

fabric requirements & cutting instructions

Read all instructions before beginning and use ¼"-wide seam allowances throughout. Read Cutting the Strips and Pieces on page 108 prior to cutting fabrics.

Country Paths Lap Quilt 60" x 72"	FIRST CUT		SECOND CUT	
	Number of Strips or Pieces	Dimensions	Number of Pieces	Dimensions
Fabric A Block Center ½ yard	3	4½" x 42"	20	4½" squares
Fabric B Center Corners ½ yard	5	2½" x 42"	80	2½" squares
Fabric C Block Diagonals 1⅞ yards	25	2½" x 42"	400	2½" squares
Fabric D Block Triangles ⅞ yard	10	2½" x 42"	80	2½" x 4½"
Fabric E Sashing 1½ yards	8 5	4½" x 42" 2½" x 42"	31 18	4½" x 8½" 2½" x 8½"
Fabric F Corner Setting Blocks ½ yard	2 2	4½" x 42" 2½" x 42"	12 14 4	4½" squares 2½" x 4½" 2½" squares

BORDERS

First Border ¼ yard	6	1" x 42"		
Second Border ⅓ yard	6	1½" x 42"		
Outside Border 1 yard	7	4½" x 42"		
Binding ⅝ yard	7	2¾" x 42"		

Backing - 3¾ yards
Batting - 66" x 78"

country paths lap quilt
finished size: 60" x 72"
photo: opposite page

getting started

This quilt consists of twenty blocks and pieced sashing. Refer to Accurate Seam Allowance on page 108. All blocks measure 8½" square, unfinished. Use the Assembly Line Method on page 108 whenever possible. Press seams in direction of arrows.

making the blocks

1. Refer to Quick Corner Triangles on page 108. Sew two 2½" Fabric B squares to opposite corners of 4½" Fabric A square as shown. Press. Repeat to sew two 2½" Fabric B squares to remaining two corners. Press. Make twenty.

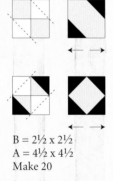

B = 2½ x 2½
A = 4½ x 4½
Make 20

2. Making quick corner triangle units, sew two 2½" Fabric C squares to 2½" x 4½" Fabric D piece as shown. Press. Make eighty.

C = 2½ x 2½
D = 2½ x 4½
Make 80

3. Sew unit from step 1 between two units from step 2 as shown. Press seams open. Make twenty.

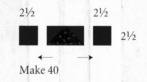

Make 20

4. Sew one unit from step 2 between two 2½" Fabric C squares. Press. Make forty.

2½   2½

          2½

Make 40

5. Sew unit from step 3 between two units from step 4 as shown. Press seams open. Make twenty. Block measures 8½" square.

Make 20
Block measures 8½" square

assembly

1. Making quick corner triangle units, sew two 2½" Fabric C squares to 2½" x 8½" Fabric E piece as shown. Press. Make eighteen.

C = 2½ x 2½
E = 2½ x 8½
Make 18

2. Making quick corner triangle units, sew two 2½" Fabric C squares to opposite corners of 4½" x 8½" Fabric E piece as shown. Press. Repeat to sew two 2½" Fabric C squares to remaining two corners. Press. Make thirty-one.

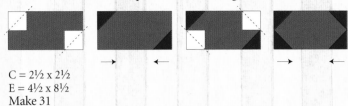

C = 2½ x 2½
E = 4½ x 8½
Make 31

3. Sew two units from step 1, four blocks from step 5, and three units from step 2 as shown to make block rows. Press. Make five rows.

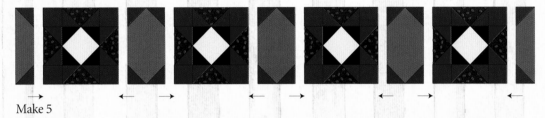

Make 5

4. Sew two 2½" x 4½" Fabric F pieces, four units from step 2, and three 4½" Fabric F squares as shown to make sashing rows. Press. Make four rows.

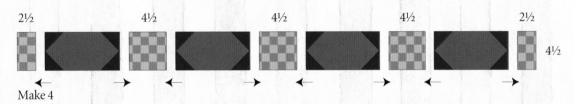

Make 4

5. Referring to photo and layout on pages 46 and 47, sew together block rows from step 3, and sashing rows from step 4, beginning and ending with block rows. Press.

6. Sew two 2½" Fabric F squares, four units from step 1, and three 2½" x 4½" Fabric F pieces as shown. Press. Make two.

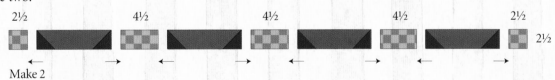

Make 2

7. Refer to photo and layout on pages 46 and 47 to sew rows from step 6 to top and bottom of quilt top. Press.

borders

1. Sew 1" x 42" First Border strips end-to-end to make one continuous 1"-wide strip. Refer to Adding the Borders on page 110. Measure quilt through center from side to side. Cut two 1"-wide border strips to that measurement. Sew to top and bottom of quilt. Press seams toward border.

2. Measure quilt through center from top to bottom, including borders just added. Cut two 1"-wide First Border strips to that measurement. Sew to sides of quilt. Press.

3. Refer to steps 1 and 2 to join, measure, trim, and sew 1½"-wide Second Border strips and 4½"-wide Outside Border strips to top, bottom, and sides of quilt. Press seams toward border.

layering & finishing

1. Cut backing fabric in half crosswise. Sew pieces together to make one 67" x 80" (approximate) backing piece. Press. Arrange and baste backing, batting, and top together, referring to Layering the Quilt on page 110.

2. Hand or machine quilt as desired.

3. Sew 2¾" x 42" binding strips end-to-end to make one continuous 2¾"-wide strip. Refer to Binding the Quilt on page 111 and bind quilt to finish.

simple four-patch

pillows

Finished sizes: 14" square, 10" square, and 5" square
Elaborate trims disguise the sewing simplicity of these charming pillows.
Simple four-patch blocks are dressed up with tassels, beads, and buttons.
Two four-patch blocks are laid one on top of the other for the larger pillow.

fabric requirements & cutting instructions

Read all instructions before beginning and use ¼"-wide seam allowances throughout. Read Cutting the Strips and Pieces on page 108 prior to cutting fabrics.

Simple Four-Patch Pillows 14" square	FIRST CUT	
	Number of Pieces	Dimensions
Fabric A Large Pillow Front	1*	7½" square
Assorted scraps in four fabrics	*Cut for each of four fabrics	
Fabric B Four-Patch Accent**	1*	3" square
Assorted scraps in four fabrics	*Cut for each of four fabrics	

Backing - One 14½" square and one 5½" square
Batting - 16½" square and 5½" square
Lining - 16½" square
Polyester Fiberfill
Four 2" Tassels
Assorted Beads & Buttons
Perle Cotton or Crochet Thread
** Or use to make 5" pillow

Simple Four-Patch Pillows 10" square	FIRST CUT	
	Number of Strips or Pieces	Dimensions
Fabric C Pillow Front*	1*	5½" squares
Assorted scraps in four fabrics	*Cut for each of four fabrics	

Backing - 10½" square
Batting - 12½" square
Lining - 12½" square
Polyester Fiberfill
Assorted Beads & Buttons
Decorative Fringe - 3½"-wide x ⅝ yard
Perle Cotton or Crochet Thread

getting started

Add elegance with these easily constructed pillows, embellish with beads and buttons. Directions are for 14" and 10" four-patch scrappy pillows. Press seams in direction of arrows. Follow same procedure to make 5" pillow using four 3" Fabric B squares.

making the 14" pillow

1. Sew two 7½" Fabric A squares together using assorted colors as shown. Press. Make two.

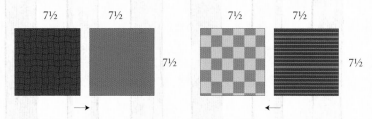

2. Sew units from step 1 together as shown. Press.

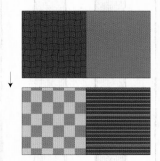

3. Layer lining, 16½" batting, and pillow top together. Baste and quilt in-the-ditch or as desired. Trim batting and lining even with pillow top.

4. For Four-Patch Accent, repeat steps 1 and 2, substituting 3" Fabric B squares.

5. Layer unit from step 4 and 5½" backing square right sides together on batting. Using a ¼"-wide seam, stitch around edges leaving a 3" opening for turning. Clip corners, turn right side out, and press. Hand-stitch opening closed.

6. Referring to photo on page 50, place Four-Patch Accent in center of 14" pillow top, matching points to seam lines. Refer to Embroidery Stitch Guide on page 110 and blind stitch in place.

7. Place pillow top and 14½" backing square right sides together. Using a ¼"-wide seam, stitch around edges leaving a 6" opening for turning. Clip corners, turn right side out, and press.

8. Stuff pillow to desired fullness with polyester fiberfill. Hand-stitch opening closed.

9. Mark the center of pillow, both front and back. Thread needle with perle cotton or crochet thread. Bring needle from center back of pillow to pillow front at center mark, leave a 5" tail. Taking a stitch approximately ¼" away, insert needle from front to back. Pull threads at back of pillow to draw center of pillow together and tie. (Technique shown on 5" pillow below.)

10. Select buttons in graduated sizes and with interesting edge treatments. Stack buttons with a bead on top and sew to pillow's center.

11. Arrange and sew seven beads around center buttons as shown. Referring to photo on page 50, sew four beads, one to each corner, on Four-Patch Accent.

12. Referring to photo on page 50, attach tassels to pillow corners.

making the 10" pillow

1. Sew two 5½" squares together using assorted colors as shown. Press. Make two.

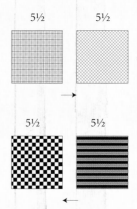

2. Sew units from step 1 together as shown. Press.

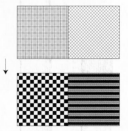

3. Layer lining, batting, and pillow top together. Baste and quilt in-the-ditch or as desired. Trim batting and lining even with pillow top.

4. Refer to photo on page 50 to arrange and sew tassel trim to pillow top.

5. Place pillow top and 10½" square backing fabric right sides together. Using a ¼"-wide seam, stitch around edges, being careful not to catch tassel trim in seam, and leave a 5" opening for turning. Clip corners, turn right side out, and press.

6. Stuff pillow to desired fullness with polyester fiberfill. Hand-stitch opening closed.

7. Mark the center of pillow both front and back. Thread needle with perle cotton or crochet thread. Referring to photo in step 9 on page 52, bring needle from back of pillow to front at center marks, leaving a 5" tail. Taking a stitch approximately ¼" away, insert needle from front to back. Pull threads at back of pillow to draw center of pillow together and tie.

8. Arrange, stack, and sew two graduated buttons and one bead to center of pillow.

decorating with sewing collectibles

Display the things you love! Favorite sewing collectibles add high style to a bookcase when carefully grouped and arranged. This display definitely says "a quilter lives here!"

Add sewing style to a bookcase with a delightful display of your favorite collectibles. A black, gold, and red color scheme ties this grouping together, providing unity and harmony to the arrangement. When set against the white background, each element stands out, yet blends together for a balanced appearance.

bottom shelf

On the bottom shelf, an antique crazy quilt block is framed in black to draw attention to this vintage piece. Framing a portion of a quilt is a great way to salvage decorative pieces from a very worn, tattered quilt. A vintage embroidery piece is also framed, preserving it for posterity. When framing vintage textiles, always use archival quality products and glass that provides UV protection. Old lace, doilies, or pieces of vintage embroidered linens can also be framed.

Anchoring the bottom shelf arrangement is a soft gold cloth with heavy fringe. A reproduction spool case is topped by a jar of buttons and small stack of fabric tied with a ribbon. A whimsical fabric figure sits on top of a pincushion while a pottery vase adds contrasting texture and color. A jar filled with sewing paraphernalia and a teacup made into a pin-cushion complete the bottom shelf.

center shelf

The middle shelf features two framed art pieces with quilt block themes. A square jar is filled with an orderly arrangement of vintage sewing collectibles. A miniature Four-Patch Pillow rests next to the jar. An antique child's sewing machine, a tomato pincushion, and an assortment of vintage bobbins complete the shelf arrangement.

top shelf

Old books are used on the top shelf, some arranged vertically and some horizontally for interest. An apothecary jar contains more buttons and favorite fabrics are folded and stacked in a basket. Fabrics don't need to be old or collectible to use them in a display. Pick a selection of your stash favorites. A vintage tin basket and a Four-Patch Pillow anchor the top shelf.

Enjoy looking at your favorite sewing collectibles every day with a charming bookcase display.

cottage garden

Imagine walking into a garden of flowers every day with the flower-filled projects in this stunning room. From the frolicking flowers on the bed quilt to the playful picket fence headboard, to the shadowy chenille blossoms on the floor, you'll gather bouquets of compliments with these easy projects!

field of flowers
bed quilt

Finished size: 69" x 93"

Frolicking flowers are framed by trellises of smaller blossoms in this fresh and fanciful quilt that's
perfect for a girl's room. Large blocks, assembly line method, and simple borders make this
quilt as fast as it is fun. Or, make it even easier by eliminating the small flower blocks.

fabric requirements & cutting instructions

Read all instructions before beginning and use ¼"-wide seam allowances throughout. Read Cutting the Strips and Pieces on page 108 prior to cutting fabrics.

Field of Flowers Bed Quilt 69" x 93"	FIRST CUT		SECOND CUT	
	Number of Strips or Pieces	Dimensions	Number of Pieces	Dimensions
Fabric A Background & Flower A Accents 2½ yards	3	6½" x 42"	16	6½" squares
	6	4½" x 42"		
	3	3½" x 42"	28	3½" squares
	2	3" x 42"	16	3" squares
	2	2½" x 42"	28	2½" squares
	4	2" x 42"	80	2" squares
	2	1½" x 42"	28	1½" squares
Fabric B Block A Petals ¾ yard	2	5½" x 42"	14	5½" squares
	4	2½" x 42"	14	2½" x 3½"
			28	2½" squares
	1	1½" x 42"	14	1½" squares
Fabric C Block A Petals ¾ yard	2	5½" x 42"	14	5½" squares
	4	2½" x 42"	14	2½" x 3½"
			28	2½" squares
	1	1½" x 42"	14	1½" squares
Fabric D Block A Centers ⅛ yard	1	2½" x 42"	7	2½" squares
Fabric E Block B Petals ⅔ yard	7	3" x 42"	80	3" squares
Fabric F Block B Accents ⅝ yard	2	4" x 42"	16	4" squares
	7	1½" x 42"	80	1½" x 3"
Fabric G Block B Centers ⅛ yard	1	1½" x 42"	20	1½" squares
BORDERS				
First & Fourth Borders 1¼ yards	7	3½" x 42"		
	6	2½" x 42"		
Second Border ⅜ yard	7	1½" x 42"		
Third Border 1⅛ yards*	7	4½" x 42"		
Outside Border & Corner Block Border ¾ yard	8	2½" x 42"		
	3	1" x 42"	8	1" x 7½"
			8	1" x 6½"
Binding ⅞ yard	9	2¾" x 42"		

Backing - 5⅝ yards
Batting - 76" x 100"
* ⅛ yard added to match plaids.

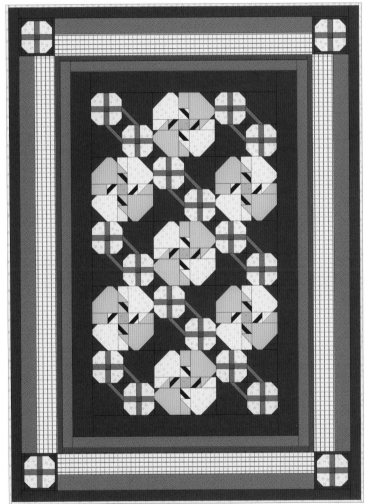

field of flowers bed quilt
finished size: 69" x 93"
photo: opposite page

getting started

This quilt consists of two flower blocks and multiple borders with corner flower blocks.

Refer to Accurate Seam Allowance on page 108 before making seven of Block A and eight of Block B. All blocks measure 12½" square, unfinished. Use the Assembly Line Method on page 108 whenever possible. Press seams in direction of arrows.

making the blocks
block A

1. Refer to Quick Corner Triangles on page 108. Sew 2½" Fabric B square to 2½" x 3½" Fabric C piece as shown. Press. Make fourteen. Making a quick corner triangle unit, sew 2½" Fabric C square to 2½" x 3½" Fabric B piece. Press. Make fourteen.

B = 2½ x 2½   C = 2½ x 2½
C = 2½ x 3½   B = 2½ x 3½
Make 14   Make 14

2. Making quick corner triangle units, sew 2½" Fabric B square to 2½" Fabric A square. Press. Sew 1½" Fabric B square to Fabric A corner on unit as shown. Press. Make fourteen.

B = 2½ x 2½
    1½ x 1½
A = 2½ x 2½
Make 14

3. Making quick corner triangle units, sew 2½" Fabric C square to 2½" Fabric A square. Press. Sew 1½" fabric C square to Fabric A corner on unit as shown. Press. Make fourteen.

C = 2½ x 2½
    1½ x 1½
A = 2½ x 2½
Make 14

make it even easier

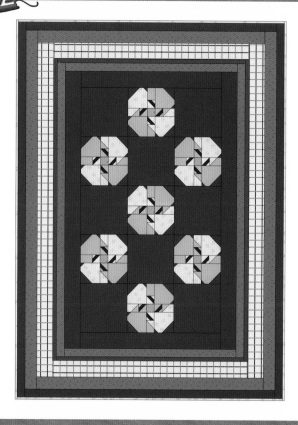

field of flowers alternative

To make this quilt even faster, use solid fabric blocks in place of Block B and eliminate the border flower blocks.

Refer to Field of Flowers Cutting Instructions

Fabric A - 2½ yards
  Eliminate:
    Three 6½" x 42" strips and pieces
    Two 3" x 42" strips and pieces
    Four 2" x 42" strips and pieces
  Cut eight 12½" squares and remaining strips and pieces for Fabric A

Eliminate Fabrics E, F & G

Cut all remaining fabrics as listed

making the quilt

1. Follow Making the Blocks (Block A) on pages 58 and 59, steps 1-9.
2. Follow Assembly on page 60, referring to Field of Flowers Alternate layout and replacing Block B with 12½" Fabric A squares.
3. Follow Borders on page 61, steps 1-4, then repeat steps 1 and 2 to measure, trim, and sew 4½"-wide Third Border, 3½"-wide Fourth Border, and 2½"-wide Outside Border to top, bottom, and sides of quilt.
4. Refer to Layering and Finishing, page 61, to complete quilt.

Capture the beauty of a field of flowers without the fuss of a lot of small pieces with this easy alternative quilt. Large flowers are featured on a field of green fabric on this colorful and captivating quilt.

4. Taking care to match colors correctly, sew unit from step 2 to first unit from step 1 as shown. Press. Sew unit from step 3 to second unit from step 1 as shown. Press. Make fourteen of each variation.

Unit 1   Unit 2

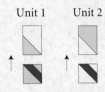

Make 14   Make 14

5. Sew 2½" Fabric D square between two of Unit 1 from step 4 as shown. Press. Make seven.

2½

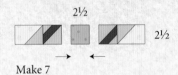

2½

Make 7

6. Making quick corner triangle units, sew 3½" and 1½" Fabric A squares to 5½" Fabric B square as shown. Press. Make fourteen.

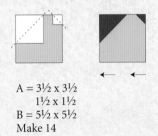

A = 3½ x 3½
    1½ x 1½
B = 5½ x 5½
Make 14

7. Making quick corner triangle units, sew 3½" and 1½" Fabric A squares to 5½" Fabric C square as shown. Press. Make fourteen.

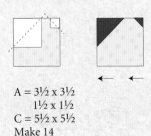

A = 3½ x 3½
    1½ x 1½
C = 5½ x 5½
Make 14

8. Sew Unit 2 from step 4 between units from steps 6 and 7, taking care to match colors correctly as shown. Press. Make fourteen.

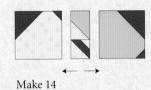

Make 14

9. Sew unit from step 5 between two units from step 8 as shown. Press. Make seven. Block measures 12½" square.

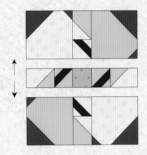

Make 7
Block measures 12½" square

block B

1. Sew 1½" x 3" Fabric F piece between two 3" Fabric E squares. Press. Make forty.

3   1½   3

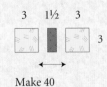

3

Make 40

2. Sew 1½" Fabric G square between two 1½" x 3" Fabric F pieces. Press. Make twenty.

3   1½   3

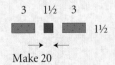

1½

Make 20

3. Sew unit from step 2 between two units from step 1. Press. Make twenty.

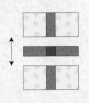

Make 20

4. Making quick corner triangle units, sew one 2" Fabric A square to each corner of unit from step 3 as shown. Press. Make twenty. Set aside four units for border.

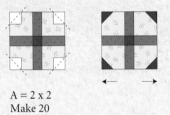

A = 2 x 2
Make 20

5. Making quick corner triangle units, sew 4" Fabric F square to 6½" Fabric A square as shown. Press. Make sixteen.

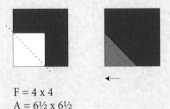

F = 4 x 4
A = 6½ x 6½
Make 16

6. Making quick corner triangle units, sew 3" Fabric A square to Fabric F corner of each unit from step 5 as shown. Press. Make sixteen.

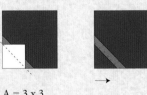

A = 3 x 3
Make 16

companion project

finished size: 20" x 30"

Welcome a sleepy head with pretty posies all in a row! Delightful in the daytime, cuddly at bedtime, these embellished pillowcases match the Field of Flowers Quilt perfectly. If machine embroidery isn't an option, try silk ribbon embroidery!

field of flowers pillowcase

Main Fabric (⅞ yard) - 26" x 40½"
Accent Strip (⅛ yard) - 1" x 40½"
Border (⅓ yard) - 8½" x 40½" *

*If machine embroidering the border, we recommend embroidering on a 12½" x 42" strip (½ yard), then cutting to 8½" x 40½" piece as shown in step 3. If making a plain pillowcase or embroidering after construction, skip to step 4.

For an alternate embroidery, refer to Embroidery Stitch Guide and Daisy Template on page 110. Using 2mm embroidery ribbon, stitch a Lazy Daisy Stitch for the petals and leaves, a French Knot for the center, and a Stem Stitch for the stem. Sew stitches loosely to give added dimension to the flowers.

making the pillowcase

1. Mark a line 5" from one long side of border fabric. Center embroidery template on marked line, 13" from short side as shown.

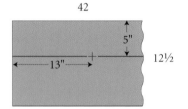

+ = Embroidery Center Placement

2. Refer to manufacturer's machine embroidery guide to place stabilizer and border fabric in hoop. We used **The Good Life by Debbie Mumm® embroidery card by Bernina® and a Bernina artista 200E and sewed two of No. 41, Aster Border,** in a mega hoop. Thread colors reflect fabrics in our quilt. Embroider border as desired.

3. Trim embroidered border to 8½" x 40½". Center of embroidery will be 10¾" from short edge and 2" from long edge of border as shown. Fold border in half lengthwise and press to mark fold line for step 7. Unfold.

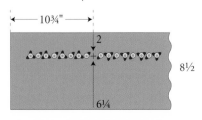

4. Sew 1" x 40½" Accent Strip between 26" x 40½" Main Fabric and 8½" x 40½" Border as shown. Press.

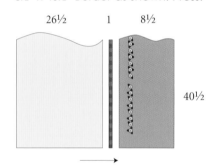

5. Fold pillowcase, right sides together, matching seams. Sew bottom edge and side seam with a ¼"-wide seam as shown.

6. Turn raw edge of border under ¼" and press as shown.

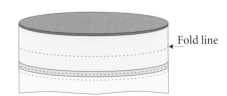

Fold line

7. Fold border, wrong sides together, over itself and Accent Strip, covering seam allowances. Press. Hand or machine stitch in place. Turn pillowcase right side out. Press.

7. Sew unit from step 4 to unit from step 6 as shown. Press. Make sixteen.

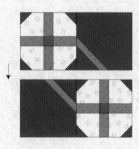

Make 16

8. Sew units from step 7 together in pairs as shown. Press. Make eight. Block measures 12½" square.

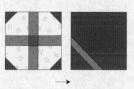

Make 8
Block measures 12½" square

assembly

1. Refer to photo and layout on pages 56 and 57. Arrange and sew Blocks A and B in five horizontal rows of three blocks each, alternating positions from row to row. Press seams in opposite directions from row to row.

2. Sew rows together. Press.

tip | decorating tip

Wallpapers and borders featured in the Cottage Garden room are from the Debbie Mumm® Collection by Imperial. Visit www.ihdg.com or your local wallpaper store.

borders

1. Sew 4½" x 42" Fabric A strips together end-to-end to make one continuous 4½"-wide strip. Referring to Adding the Borders on page 110, measure quilt through center from side to side. Cut two 4½"-wide strips to that measurement. Sew to top and bottom of quilt. Press toward border.

2. Measure quilt through center from top to bottom including the borders just added. Cut two 4½"-wide strips to that measurement. Sew to sides of quilt. Press toward border.

3. Repeat steps 1 and 2 to sew 2½"-wide First Border and 1½"-wide Second Border to quilt. Press toward borders.

4. Sew 4½"-wide Third Border strips together end-to-end to make one continuous 4½"-wide strip. Repeat to sew 3½"-wide Fourth Border strips together. Press.

5. Sew the Third and Fourth Border strips together lengthwise to make a border strip set, staggering seams. Press toward Fourth Border.

6. Measure through center of the quilt from side to side and cut two strips to this length. Measure through center of quilt from top to bottom. Cut two strips to this measurement and set aside. Referring to layout on page 57, sew short border strip sets to top and bottom of quilt. Press toward borders.

7. Sew Block B unit from step 4 between two 1" x 6½" Outside Border pieces. Press. Make four.

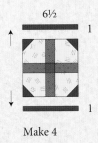

Make 4

8. Sew unit from step 7 between two 1" x 7½" Outside Border pieces Press. Make four.

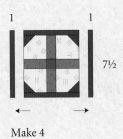

Make 4

9. Referring to photo and layout on pages 56 and 57, sew remaining long border strip sets from step 6 between two blocks from step 8 as shown. Press. Make two. Sew to sides of quilt. Press toward border.

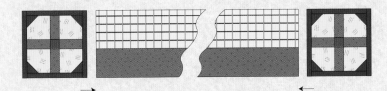

10. Repeat steps 1 and 2 to join, measure, trim, and sew 2½" x 42" Outside Border strips to quilt. Press toward border.

layering & finishing

1. Cut backing crosswise into two equal pieces and sew pieces together to make one 83" x 100" (approximate) backing piece. Press. Arrange and baste backing, batting, and top together, referring to Layering the Quilt on page 110.

2. Hand or machine quilt as desired.

3. Sew the 2¾" x 42" binding strips end-to-end to make one continuous 2¾"-wide binding strip. Refer to Binding the Quilt on page 111 and bind quilt to finish.

picket fence
headboard

Finished size: 42½" wide with pickets
Whimsical flowers peek through the pickets on this sweet and sentimental headboard,
perfect for our garden-themed room. Real fence pickets frame this easy
quilting project, or make faux pickets for an even faster approach.

fabric requirements & cutting instructions

Read all instructions before beginning and use ¼"-wide seam allowances throughout. Read Cutting the Strips and Pieces on page 108 prior to cutting fabrics.

Picket Fence Headboard Quilt 42½" x 31½"	FIRST CUT		SECOND CUT	
	Number of Strips or Pieces	Dimensions	Number of Pieces	Dimensions
Fabric A Background ⅞ yard	3	5¼" x 42"	6	5¼" x 20"
	2	3½" x 42"	1	3½" x 11"
			12	3½" squares
			1	2½" x 11"
	2	2" x 42"	6	2" x 8"
			1	1½" x 11"
Fabric B Flowers ¼ yard each of three fabrics	1*	8" squares		
	*Cut for each fabric			
Fabric C Stems ⅛ yard	2	1½" x 42"	3	1½" x 20"
Fabric D Fence 1¼ yards directional** OR 1 yard non-directional	3	42" x 2¾" Top and side bindings		
	1	42" x 2½" Top border		
	4	27" x 3" Pickets		
Fabric E Prairie Points ⅙ yard each of five fabrics	4*	4½" squares		
	*Cut for each fabric			
Fabric F ¼ yard	1	2¾" x 42" Bottom binding		
	1	2½" x 42" Bottom border		

Flower Ruffles - Assorted scraps
Leaf Appliqués - ¼ yard
Backing - 1⅓ yards
Batting - 47" x 37"
Three 1¼" Buttons for flower centers
For picket fence, refer to page 67

**For directional fabric the measurement that is listed first runs parallel to selvage (strip width).*

picket fence headboard quilt
42½" x 31½" without wooden pickets
photo: opposite page

getting started

You will be making three flower sections. Each section measures 11" x 27" unfinished. A fabric picket borders each section. Refer to Accurate Seam Allowance on page 108 before making blocks. Use the Assembly Line Method on page 108 whenever possible. Press seams in direction of arrows.

assembly

1. Refer to Quick Corner Triangles on page 108. Sew one 3½" Fabric A square to each corner of 8" Fabric B square as shown. Press. Make three, one of each combination.

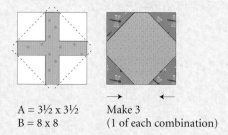

A = 3½ x 3½
B = 8 x 8

Make 3
(1 of each combination)

2. Sew unit from step 1 between two 2" x 8" Fabric A pieces. Press. Make three, one of each combination.

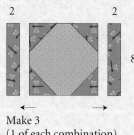

Make 3
(1 of each combination)

3. Sew units from step 2 to 3½" x 11", 1½" x 11", and 2½" x 11" Fabric A pieces as shown. Press.

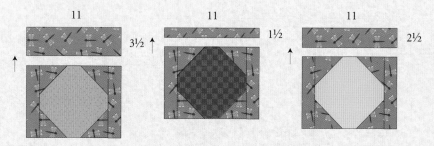

4. Sew 1½" x 20" Fabric C strip between two 5¼" x 20" Fabric A pieces. Press. Make three.

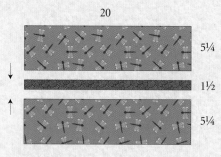

Make 3

5. Sew unit from step 4 to unit from step 3 as shown. Make three, one of each variation. Trim unit **at bottom** so each unit measures 27" long.

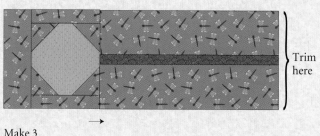

Make 3
(1 of each variation)
Trim at bottom to 27" long

6. Sew three units from step 5 and four 27" x 3" Fabric D strips as shown. Press.

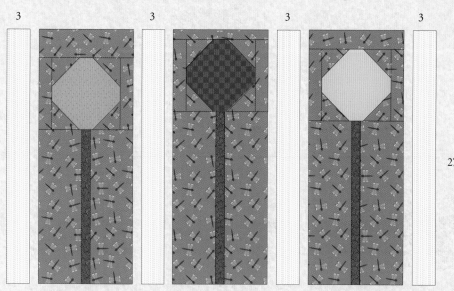

27

7. Fold 4½" Fabric E square in half once diagonally, wrong sides together. Press and fold diagonally in half once again to make Prairie Point. Press. Make nineteen.

Make 19

8. Placing raw edges at lower edge of quilt, insert single fold of each Prairie Point inside double fold of next point and arrange Prairie Points along lower edge of quilt as desired. Baste.

9. Referring to Adding the Borders on page 110, measure quilt through center from side to side. Cut 42" x 2½" Fabric D and 2½" x 42" Fabric F strips to that measurement. Sew Fabric D strip to top and Fabric F strip to bottom of quilt. Press toward border.

bouquet of flowers lamp and shade

materials needed for lamp base

Purchased wooden lamp
Acrylic paints in medium green, ivory, yellow, and orange
Assorted paintbrushes
Ruler and pencil
Antiquing medium
Matte spray varnish

materials needed for lampshade

Lampshade in appropriate size and color
Silk flower bush (such as hydrangea)
Silk leaves
Assorted beads and buttons
Heavyweight thread to match lamp shade and needle
Hot glue gun

Bring soft light and a bouquet of dainty flowers into your cottage garden room with this sweet lamp. Silk flowers, buttons, and beads decorate the shade, while bands of pretty color and charming checks highlight the lamp base.

painting the lamp base

1. Select a wooden lamp base that has an interesting design. Our lamp came from a national discount store and it was already painted a soft vanilla color with a matte finish. We chose to make painting easier by using the existing color as the background color for our lamp. If lamp has a glossy finish, it should be sanded before painting. Allow paint to dry thoroughly between each step.

2. Using the features of your lamp as a guide, determine where you will paint each color. Bands of color were painted freehand where appropriate for our lamp design, using the same colors selected for the bedside table (page 72).

3. To make a checkerboard pattern like the one shown on the lamp base, measure the area selected and use a ruler and pencil to mark two rows of checks. Paint every other check with green paint in a checkerboard fashion. Alternate checks are painted ivory.

4. When painting is complete and dry, apply a light coat of antiquing medium, following manufacturer's directions. Wipe off almost all antiquing medium, allowing antiquing to remain in indentations. When antiquing is thoroughly dry, spray lamp base with several coats of varnish, following manufacturer's directions.

embellishing the lampshade

Select a silk flower bush that has many small flowers that can be individually pulled off the bush. The silk bush we used was a hydrangea and the small individual flowers had four petals each. The silk leaves were also on a bush and were cut off to be applied individually to the lampshade. Both silk bushes came from a national craft store.

1. Use hot glue gun to affix silk leaves around the bottom of the lampshade as shown in photo. Make sure glue is not used in the area where flowers are desired.

2. Flowers, buttons, and beads were sewn on, stitching through buttons and beads to hold silk flowers in place. A continuous length of thread, with large stitches between flowers, made this process easy. If desired, flowers can be hot glued on, but beads and buttons require a stronger adhesive such as E6000®.

As buttons and beads can present a choking hazard, this lampshade is not recommended for small children.

layering &finishing

1. Arrange and baste backing, batting, and top together referring to Layering the Quilt on page 110.

2. Hand or machine quilt as desired. If you choose to eliminate the wooden fence frame, refer to Make It Even Easier (page 67) at this point to add fabric hanging tabs, if desired.

3. Referring to Binding the Quilt on page 111, sew 42" x 2¾" Fabric D binding strip to top of quilt. Press. Sew 2¾" x 42" Fabric F to bottom of quilt. Press. Then sew 42" x 2¾" Fabric D binding strips to sides of quilt and bind.

4. For Flower Ruffles, trace three 5" and three 4" circles onto wrong side of fabric scraps using the Circle Templates on page 102. Place marked circle right sides together on top of matching size scrap. Stitch on drawn line. Cut out circle, leaving a ³⁄₁₆"-wide seam allowance. On back of circle, make small slit for turning, as shown. Notch around seam allowance, turn, and press.

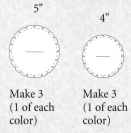

5" — Make 3 (1 of each color)

4" — Make 3 (1 of each color)

5. At center of each 5" circle, run a line of basting stitches 1¼" in diameter, as shown. Pull slightly to gather and tie off. Repeat with 4" circles, running basting stitches 1" in diameter. Tack large, then small circles to center of flowers on quilt. Attach 1¼" button to center of each flower.

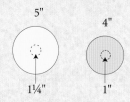

5"

4"

1¼"

1"

Basting Stitches

6. For Leaves, trace six leaves onto wrong side of fabric using the template below. Place marked leaves right sides together on top of matching size fabric. Stitch on drawn lines. Cut out leaves, leaving a ³⁄₁₆"-wide seam allowance. On back of leaf, make small slit for turning. Clip curves, turn, and press.

7. Referring to photo and layout on pages 62 and 63, arrange and pin leaves to quilt. With sewing machine, triple stitch through all layers along the center of each leaf and vein lines to attach leaves. If you prefer hand embroidery, refer to Embroidery Stitches on page 110 and use a stem stitch to embellish leaves.

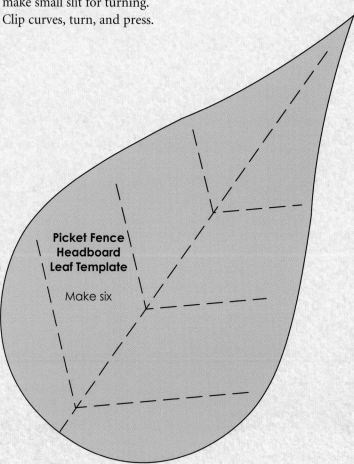

Picket Fence Headboard Leaf Template

Make six

constructing the picket fence headboard

MATERIALS NEEDED

Wooden Gothic Pickets -
    1" x 4" x 42"

Cedar board - Eight feet of
    1" x 3" boards

Sandpaper

Ivory acrylic paint

Paintbrush

Sixteen nails

Eight decorative upholstery tacks

Matte spray varnish

Wood finish*

Eight thumbtacks

*Check with your local hardware store for
an appropriate wood finish, such as
polyurethane, polyacrylic, or high build
epoxy coating.

1. Referring to photo on page 62, arrange pickets and boards on quilt to determine desired lengths. Cut boards and pickets to desired length. Sand and remove residue with tack cloth or damp rag. Paint with ivory paint. Allow to dry. Sand pickets again to give wood a distressed look. Apply matte varnish to all surfaces.

2. Arrange pickets and boards and nail together, using two nails at top and base of each picket as shown in photo on page 62.

3. Coat back of cross pieces with appropriate wood finish to seal the wood. Allow to dry thoroughly. This step is necessary, as inappropriately finished wood will damage fabric.

4. Referring to photo, position and tack decorative tacks to pickets.

5. Carefully push thumb tacks into back of quilt, working points between threads in weave. Push thumb tacks into back of wooden cross pieces to attach quilt to frame.

6. Attach headboard to bed frame or hang from wall.

make it even easier ez

picket fence alternative

Finished size: 42½" x 34½"

Fabric D - Scraps (page 63)
    four 9½" x 5½"
Eight ⅜" buttons

1. Refer to Cutting Instructions on page 63. Complete Picket Fence Headboard steps 1-9 on page 64 through step 2 on page 66.
2. Fold 9½" x 5½" Fabric D strips in half lengthwise, right sides together. Stitch along 9½" edge. Center seam along back and press seam allowance open as shown. Stitch across one end. Clip corners, turn, and press. Make four.

3. Place tabs, with raw edges aligned, at top on back of quilt. Make sure tabs are aligned with pickets. Pin or baste in place.
4. Continue with Layering and Finishing, page 66, steps 3 and 4. Be careful not to catch tabs in side bindings.
5. Referring to photo, fold tabs to front of quilt, placing edge at bottom of top border. Fasten each tab to quilt with two ⅜" buttons, if desired.
6. Insert a curtain rod through tabs to hang.

Fabric tabs fastened with button "nails" will give
the look of pickets without the lumber!

Make 4

carpet of flowers
chenille rug

Finished size: 24" x 36"
Soft chenille will cozy your toes when you make this sturdy yet stunning rug
to accent the Cottage Garden boudoir. Simple marking, stitching, and
cutting techniques make this project much easier than it looks!

Carpet of Flowers 24" x 36"	FIRST CUT	
	Number of Strips or Pieces	Dimensions
Fabric A Background 1½ yards	2	24½" x 36½"
Fabric B Chenille Layers 2⅛ yards	3	24½" x 36½"
Fabric C Flowers ¼ yard each of three fabrics	1*	8" square
	*Cut for each fabric	
Fabric D Stems ⅛ yard	1 1 1	1" x 15½" 1" x 14½" 1" x 13½"
Flower Centers Assorted scraps	3 3	4" squares 2" squares
Grass Assorted scraps	18	2" squares

Leaves - ⅛ yard
Cotton Backing and Chenille underlayer - 1⅔ yards
Batting - 27" x 39"
Washable Glue Stick
Slash Cutter or Blunt-Nose Scissors
Rug Webbing** - 4 yards
Non-Skid Rug Pad - 22" x 34"

** If you prefer to bind the rug, use ⅜ yard fabric and cut four 2¾" x 42" strips.

getting started

This rug is fast to make as the rug is quilted and the chenille is sewn in one step. Read all instructions before beginning.

The final look and texture in a chenille rug is determined by the variety of colors and number of fabrics used in layering*. For an impressionistic look, use a neutral color fabric for all layers except the background. We used two background layers to add a strong background color to the rug. Seams for the rug are stitched every ⅜" to soften the appearance and texture.

Pre-wash fabric only if you are concerned with color bleeding. The rug will shrink considerably after wetting and drying, which enhances the chenille look.

* This rug consists of the following layers:

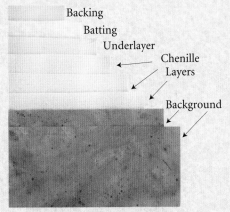

Backing
Batting
Underlayer
Chenille Layers
Background

After stitching, all layers except backing, batting, and underlayer, are cut to form chenille.

assembling the layers

Note: When stitching chenille, use a walking foot on your machine to make smoother stitching lines.

1. To prepare backing and underlayer for chenille, cut two 27" x 39" pieces. Using a 45° mark on a ruler, draw a diagonal line on right side of one 27" x 39" piece from top to lower left corner as shown. This will be the backing for the rug.

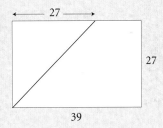

2. Continue drawing 45° angle lines ¾" apart on both sides of line drawn in step 1 as shown. To achieve ⅜"-wide seams, draw lines between ¾" lines, if desired, but we found it easier to only mark ¾"-wide lines and sew an extra seam between drawn lines.

3. Place batting and underlayer on unmarked side of backing fabric. Center three 24½" x 36½" Fabric B pieces and two 24½" x 36½" Fabric A pieces on underlayer. Pin at corners to anchor.

4. Using rotary cutter and 45° mark on ruler, cut 3" triangle off each corner of 8" Fabric C square as shown. Make one in each of three colors.

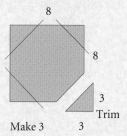

Make 3

5. Using Leaf Template below, cut three leaves and three reversed.

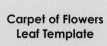

**Carpet of Flowers
Leaf Template**

Cut three and three reversed.

6. Position Flower, Flower Center, Stem, Leaf, and Grass pieces on background, as shown. Overlap stems by ½" with Flowers.

7. Apply glue stick to the back of each piece and hand-press in place. Ensure that edges of each piece adhere to background. It is best to stitch chenille as soon as fabric pieces are glued, or hand baste edges in place.

8. Turn layered piece over so marked backing is up. Pin to secure layers as needed, remove any pins from other side.

9. Stitch through all layers using 2.5-3 mm stitch-length (10-12 stitches per inch), starting on first drawn line. Continue stitching parallel lines, reversing the direction of stitching for each line as shown, until all lines are stitched. Periodically check the other side to make sure all pieces are fastened in the correct position.

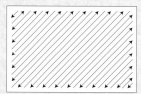

10. Turn rug over to right side. Use a slash cutter or blunt-nose scissors to cut through chenille layers, including background fabric and all flower pieces. Be careful to avoid cutting underlayer, batting, and backing.

11. Thoroughly wet rug with cold water, towel dry, and place in a dryer with towel to fluff and thoroughly dry chenille. If desired, the rug may be brushed with a chenille brush to roughen and fluff raw edges.

12. Trim underlayer, batting, and backing to within ¼" of chenille. Using ¼"-wide seam allowance, attach rug webbing to right side of top and bottom of rug. Press webbing away from rug top being careful to avoid pressing chenille. Sew webbing to sides of rug, including webbing just added. Press. Fold top and bottom webbing to back of rug, then repeat with sides. Press and pin in position. Hand stitch in place. Or, cut four 2¾"-wide Binding strips, sew end-to-end, and refer to Binding the Quilt on page 111 to bind edges.

13. Place a 22" x 34" non-skid pad under rug to prevent slipping.

perfect flower pillow

finished size: 18" square

Fabric A (Background) - ⅝ yard
  One 18" square
Fabric B (Chenille Layers) -1⅛ yards
  Three 18" squares
Flower - Scrap
  One 8" square
Flower Centers - Scraps
  One 4" square, one 2" square
Stem - Scrap
  One 1" x 9½" piece
Leaves - Scrap
  One 2½" x 12" piece
Border - Assorted scraps
  Eighteen 2" squares
Backing and Underlayer - ⅝ yards
  Two 20" squares
Batting - 20" square
Washable glue stick
Pillow Backing - ½ yard
  Two 12" x 18" pieces
Pillow Form - 18" square
Slash cutter or blunt-nose scissors

One perfect flower is shown in all its glory on this simple chenille pillow. Lines are stitched every half inch to simplify the process and achieve a slightly different chenille look.

making the pillow

1. On right side of 20" Backing square, draw a 45°-angle line from top right corner to lower left corner. Continue drawing parallel lines every ½" on both sides of center line. Diagram is for example only. You will have approximately forty-seven lines.

Draw approximately 47 lines

2. Place batting and underlayer on unmarked side of backing fabric. Center three 18" Fabric B squares and 18" Fabric A square on underlayer. Pin corners to hold in place.

3. Refer to Chenille Rug, page 70, step 4, to cut Flower. Using Leaf Template on page 70, cut one leaf and one reversed.

4. Refer to Carpet of Flowers steps 7-11, pages 70-71, and photo to glue, quilt, and make chenille for pillow.

5. Trim backing, batting, and underlayer to within ¼" of chenille.

6. Use 12" x 18" Pillow Backing pieces and refer to Making Pillows, steps 2-4, on page 111 to finish pillow.

garden basket
bedside table

A flower-filled room, brimming with beautiful colors and textures, will be even more
inviting with a bedside table that continues the garden theme. Purchased placemats
used as wicker accents and easy painting techniques make this table as quick as it is cute!

Garden Basket Bedside Table

MATERIALS NEEDED

Purchased bedside table

Acrylic paints in ivory, medium yellow, light yellow, dark green, medium green, and orange

Assorted paintbrushes

Sea sponge

Woven wicker placemats

Decorative molding (½"-wide)

Two flower buttons (optional)

Heavy duty adhesive such as E6000®

Sandpaper

Tack cloth or damp rag

Finishing nails and hammer

Miter box and saw

Pencil and tape measure

Matte spray varnish

make it even easier

easier alternatives

There are several ways to make this project even easier. Get the look of wicker without having to cut moldings by using decoupage to affix a printed wicker scrapbook paper or fabric onto the drawer fronts. Finish edges with paint. Instead of painting a dragonfly, use a dragonfly stencil or rubber stamp, or, use a dragonfly sticker and apply decoupage over it for permanent coverage.

painting the bedside table

1. Sand all surfaces to remove gloss and oils from any existing finish. Use a tack cloth or damp rag to remove residue.

2. Using the design features of your bedside table as a guide, determine placement of paint and wicker accents. We chose to apply the wicker accents to the drawers and to the sides of our table. Other areas were selected for green stipple, soft yellow stipple, and solid ivory painting techniques.

3. Remove drawers from bedside table. Cut woven wicker placemats about ¼" less on all sides than the size needed to completely cover drawer fronts. Decorative molding will go over the edges of the wicker. Measure carefully and use a miter box and saw to cut decorative moldings to size, forming a frame that is flush with drawer edges, as shown in photo. Paint moldings in the desired color. Set moldings and wicker inserts aside to be finished later. If desired, prepare wicker accents and moldings for sides of bedside table as well.

4. Using photo as a guide, paint sides of bedside table with the dark green paint. Two coats of paint may be required for good coverage. Allow to dry between coats. Place a small amount of dark green paint and medium green paint on a palette or paper plate. Wet sea sponge with water and wring thoroughly. Dip sea sponge in both colors of paint and sponge color over the dark green paint using a tapping motion. Use a light touch for a lightly stippled effect. Allow to dry.

5. Paint top in the same way using medium yellow as your basecoat and sponge with the medium yellow and light yellow paints. Allow to dry.

6. Use ivory paint where desired. We used ivory for the edge of the top, the drawer moldings, and inset areas on our bedside table. Allow to dry thoroughly. If desired, add a dragonfly to front of bedside table as shown in detail photo. Use ends of paint brushes to form dots for the dragonfly body.

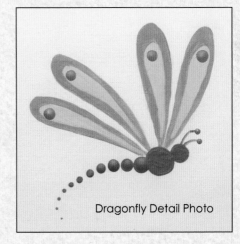

Dragonfly Detail Photo

7. Using heavy duty adhesive, glue wicker accents from step 3 to drawer fronts and sides, if desired. Use finishing nails to tack pre-painted moldings in place.

8. When everything is thoroughly dry, spray with several coats of matte varnish, following manufacturer's directions.

9. If desired, glue flower buttons to drawer pulls using heavy-duty adhesive.

sleeping under the stars

A lucky child will sleep under the stars every night at this indoor campsite! From the soft and cozy star-studded bed quilt, to the unique "tent" headboard, to the laced logs bulletin board, your child will camp out every night in the comfort you created.

star gazer
bed quilt

Finished size: 70½" x 95½"
A special child will sleep under the stars every night and enjoy the soft flannel feel every
day when you make this cozy quilt. A unique technique creates the
stars without set-in seams and easy big stitch quilting will make finishing fast!

fabric requirements & cutting instructions

Read all instructions before beginning and use ¼"-wide seam allowances throughout. Read Cutting the Strips and Pieces on page 108 prior to cutting fabrics.

Star Gazer Bed Quilt 70½" x 95½"	FIRST CUT		SECOND CUT	
	Number of Strips	Dimensions	Number of Pieces	Dimensions
Fabric A Background 1¾ yards*	1	23½" x 42"	1	23½" x 3½"
			1	17½" x 10½"
			2	17½" x 6½"
			2	17½" x 4½"
	1	15½" x 42"	1	15½" x 4½"
			1	13½" x 8½"
			1	13½" x 6½"
			1	12½" x 5½"
			2	12½" x 3½"
			2	12½" x 2½"
	1	11½" x 42"	1	11½" x 17½"
			4	9½" x 4½"
	1	6½" x 42"	1	6½" x 17½"
			1	6½" x 12½"
Fabric B Block Corner Triangles 1½ yards	3	9⅜" x 42"	10**	9⅜" squares
	2	7" x 42"	6**	7" squares
	1	5½" x 42"	6**	5½" squares
			** Cut once diagonally	
Fabric C Star Background ¾ yard	2	7" x 42"	10	7" squares
	1	5¼" x 42"	6	5¼" squares
	1	4¼" x 42"	6	4¼" squares
Fabric D Large Star Accent Points ½ yard	2	7" x 42"	10	7" squares
Fabric E Lg Star Points ⅞ yard	4	6¾" x 42"	20	6¾" squares
Fabric F Medium and Small Star Accent Points ⅓ yard	1	5¼" x 42"	6	5¼" squares
	1	4¼" x 42"	6	4¼" squares
Fabric G Medium Star Points ⅜ yard	2	5" x 42"	12	5" squares
Fabric H Small Star Points ⅓ yard	2	4" x 42"	12	4" squares

BORDERS

First Border ⅝ yard	7	2½" x 42"		
Second Border ½ yard	7	1¾" x 42"		
Outside Border 1⅞ yards	8	7½" x 42"		
Binding ¾ yard	9	2¾" x 42"		

Backing - 5¾ yards
Batting - 78" x 103"

*For directional fabric the measurement listed first runs parallel to selvage (strip width).

star gazer bed quilt
finished size: 70½" x 95½"
photo: opposite page

getting started

You will be making Star Blocks in three different sizes: 17½" square, 12½" square, and 9½" square unfinished. There are five Large Star Blocks, three Medium Star Blocks, and three Small Star Blocks. Labeling each Star Block and each assembly unit for sections as indicated will make construction easier. Refer to Accurate Seam Allowance on page 108 before making blocks. Use the Assembly Line Method on page 108 whenever possible. Press seams in direction of arrows.

making the blocks

1. Draw a diagonal line on wrong side of 7" Fabric C square. Place one Fabric C square on one 7" Fabric D square, right sides together. Sew a scant ¼" away from drawn line on both sides to make half-square triangles as shown. Make ten. Cut on drawn line. Press ten units toward Fabric C and ten units toward Fabric D to make twenty half-square triangle units. Square to 6½".

C = 7 x 7
D = 7 x 7
Make 10

Make 20
Square to 6½"

2. Fold 6¾" Fabric E square in half diagonally with wrong sides together. Stitch ¼" seam along one side as shown. Align seam in center of piece as shown and press seam open. Trim excess seam allowance at point as shown. Make twenty.

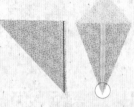

Trim seam allowance

3. Arrange unit from step 2 on top of unit from step 1, matching raw edges at corner as shown. Edge-stitch 1/16" from folded edge as shown. Make twenty.

4. Sew units from step 3 together in pairs as shown, matching opposing seams. Press. Make ten.

Make 10

5. Sew units from step 4 together in pairs as shown. Press seam open. Make five.

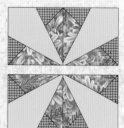

Make 5

6. Sew unit from step 5 between two 9⅜" Fabric B triangles. Press. Sew two 9⅜" Fabric B triangles to remaining sides of unit as shown. Press. Make five. Block measures 17½" square. Label these blocks Large Star.

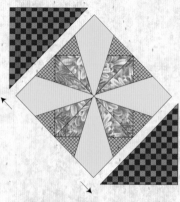

Make 5
Block measures 17½" square

companion project

7. Repeat step 1, using 5¼" Fabric C and Fabric F squares to make half-square triangles. Make six, for a total of twelve half-square triangle units. Press six units toward Fabric C and six units toward Fabric F. Square to 4¾".

C = 5¼ x 5¼
F = 5¼ x 5¼
Make 6

Make 12
Square to 4¾"

8. Repeat steps 2 and 3 using 5" Fabric G squares. Make twelve. Using these units repeat steps 4 and 5. Press. Make three.

Make 12   Make 3

9. Sew unit from step 8 between two 7" Fabric B triangles. Press. Sew two 7" Fabric B triangles to remaining sides of unit. Press. Make three. Block measures 12½" square. Label blocks Medium Star.

Make 3
Block measures 12½" square

star gazer pillow

Fabric B (Block Corner Triangles and Background) - 1 yard
  Six 9½" squares
  Twelve 5½" squares, cut once diagonally
Fabric C (Star Background and Accent Ends) - 1⅛ yards
  Two 14½" x 36½" pieces
  Twelve 4¼" squares
Fabric F (Star Accent Points) - ⅓ yard
  Twelve 4¼" squares
Fabric H (Star Points) - ½ yard
  Twenty-four 4" squares
Cord Shoelaces - one pair 36" long
Cord Lock Fasteners - 2
Pillow Form - 1⅛ yards
  One 27½" x 36½" piece
  Two 12" Circles
Fiberfill

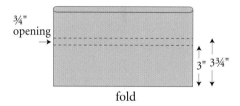

finished size: 18" x 41"

A camp wouldn't be complete without a sleeping bag! Cord cinches on each side of this pillow make it look like a sleeping bag stow sack. Stuffed with an extra pillow or small sleeping bag for overnight guests, it's as functional as it is quick to make.

making the pillow

Refer to Star Gazer Bed Quilt page 80, steps 10-12, to make six Small Star Blocks.

1. Sew one Small Star block between two 9½" Fabric B squares. Press toward Fabric B. Make two. Sew one 9½" Fabric B square between two Small Star Blocks. Press toward Fabric B. Make two.

2. Refer to photo to arrange and sew four rows from step 1 together. Press. Fold in half, right sides together, and stitch using ¼"-wide seam along the 27½" side to form a tube. Press. Turn right side out.

3. Fold 14½" x 36½" Fabric C piece crosswise, right sides together, and stitch along the 14½" side leaving a ¾" opening as shown. Back-stitch at ¾" to secure. Press seam open. Make two. Turn right side out.

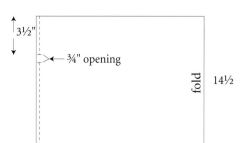

3½"

¾" opening

fold   14½

4. Fold unit from step 3 in half lengthwise, wrong sides together, matching raw edges and seam. Using a removable fabric marker, make marks 3" and 3¾" from folded edge beginning at ¾" opening. Stitch on marked lines to form casing. The right side will be the side with the ¾" opening.

¾" opening →

3" 3¾"

fold

5. Place unit from step 4 and unit from step 2, right sides together, align edges, and stitch. Press. Repeat for other side.

6. Insert shoelace through casing and attach cord lock fasteners following manufacturer's directions.

making a bolster pillow form

1. Fold 27½" x 36½" piece crosswise, right sides together. Stitch along the 36½" side, leaving a 6" opening in the center for turning later. Press seams open.

2. Pin and stitch 12" circles to each end of tube from step 1, turn right side out and fill with fiberfill. Hand-stitch opening closed. Insert into Star Gazer Pillow.

10. Repeat step 1, page 78, using 4¼" Fabric C and Fabric F squares. Make six, for a total of twelve half-square triangle units. Press six units toward Fabric C and six units toward Fabric F. Square to 3¾".

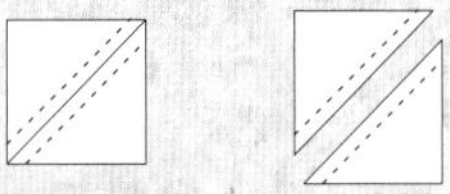

C = 4¼ x 4¼
F = 4¼ x 4¼
Make 6

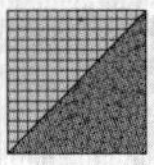

Make 12
Square to 3¾"

11. Repeat steps 2 and 3 using 4" Fabric H squares. Make twelve. Using these units repeat steps 4 and 5. Press. Make three.

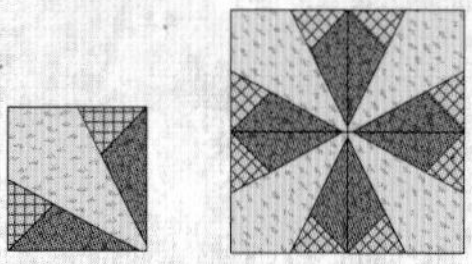

Make 12   Make 3

12. Sew unit from step 11 between two 5½" Fabric B triangles. Press. Sew two 5½" Fabric B triangles to remaining sides of unit. Press. Make three. Block measures 9½"square. Label blocks Small Star.

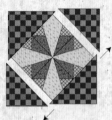

Make 3
Block measures 9½" square

13. Sew Medium Star Block, from step 9, between 12½" x 2½" and 12½" x 3½" Fabric A strips as shown. Press. Make two. Label one unit for Section 1 and one unit for Section 2.

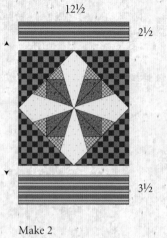

12½
2½
3½

Make 2

make it even easier

Cozy flannel fabrics and giant-size blocks make a quick quilt that anybody will love. Add a patchwork of simple blocks for an easy coordinating pillow!

quick n' cozy twin bed quilt

Finished size: 70" x 93"
Fabric A (Dark) - 2⅞ yards
    Four 23½" squares
Fabric B (Dark) - 1½ yards
    Two 23½" squares
Fabric C (Light) - 2⅞ yards
    Four 23½" squares
Fabric D (Light) - 1½ yards
    Two 23½" squares
Binding - ¾ yard
    Nine 2¾" x 42" strips
Backing - 5¾ yards

assembly

1. Sew one 23½" Fabric D square between two 23½" Fabric A squares. Press toward Fabric A. Make 2.
2. Sew one 23½" Fabric B square between two 23½" Fabric C squares. Press toward Fabric B. Make 2.
3. Refer to photo to arrange and sew four rows from steps 1 and 2 together. Press.
4. Arrange and baste backing, batting, and top together, referring to Layering the Quilt on page 110. Hand or machine quilt as desired.

5. Refer to Binding the Quilt on page 111 and bind quilt to finish.

quick n' cozy bed pillow

Fabric A (Print) - ⅝ yard
    Six 9½" squares
Fabric B (Plaid) - ⅝ yard
    Six 9½" squares
Fabric C (Accent Ends) - ⅞ yard
    Two 14½" x 36½" pieces
Cord Shoelaces - one pair 36" long
Cord Lock Fasteners - 2
Pillow Form Fabric - 1⅛ yards
Fiberfill

assembly

1. Sew one 9½" Fabric A square between two 9½" Fabric B squares. Press. Make two.
2. Sew one 9½" Fabric B square between two 9½" Fabric A squares. Press. Make two.
3. Refer to Star Gazer Pillow page 79, steps 3-6, and Making a Bolster Pillow Form to finish the pillow, steps 1 and 2.

14. Sew 9½" x 4½" Fabric A strip to Small Star Block from step 12 as shown. Press. Make three.

9½

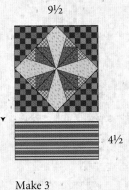

4½

Make 3

15. Sew 13½" x 8½" Fabric A piece to one unit from step 14 as shown. Press. Label for Section 2.

8½

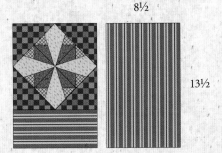

13½

16. Sew 13½" x 6½" Fabric A piece, then 15½" x 4½" Fabric A piece to one unit from step 14 as shown. Press. Label for Section 3.

15½

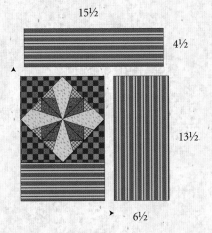

4½

13½

6½

17. Sew 9½" x 4½" Fabric A piece to remaining unit from step 14 as shown. Press. Label for Section 4.

9½

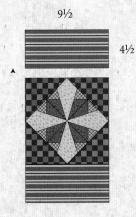

4½

18. Sew Medium Star block from step 9 between 6½" x 12½" and 12½" x 5½" Fabric A pieces as shown. Label for Section 5.

12½

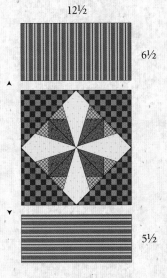

6½

5½

19. Sew 6½" x 17½" Fabric A strip to Large Star Block from step 6 as shown. Press. Label for Section 5.

17½

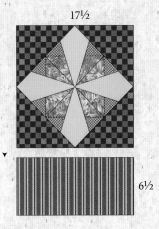

6½

assembling the sections

1. Section 1: Sew 17½" x 10½" Fabric A strip between Large Star Block and unit from step 13. Sew this unit between 17½" x 6½" and 17½" x 4½" Fabric A pieces as shown. Press.

2. Section 2: Sew unit from step 15 to unit from step 13 as shown. Sew Large Star Block between 17½" x 4½" and 11½" x 17½" Fabric A pieces, then sew to unit as shown. Press.

3. Section 3: Sew unit from step 16 to Large Star Block as shown. Press.

4. Section 4: Sew 17½" x 6½" Fabric A strip between Large Star Block and unit from step 17 as shown. Press.

5. Section 5: Sew unit from step 19 between unit from step 18 and 23½" x 3½" Fabric A strip as shown. Press.

6. Assembly: Sew Section 4 between Sections 3 and 5. Press seams toward center. Sew to Section 2. Press. Sew Section 1 to top of unit. Press.

assembly layout

Section 1

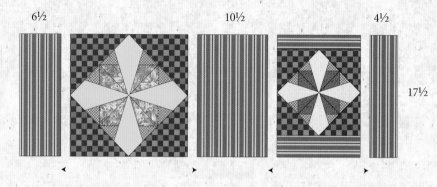

Section 2

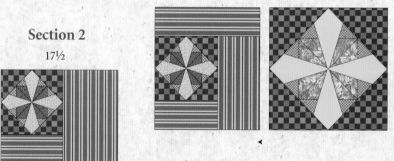

Section 3

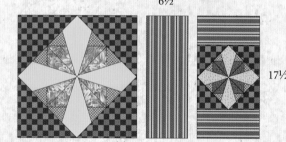

Section 4

Section 5

making the borders

1. Sew 2½" x 42" First Border strips together end-to-end to make one continuous 2½"-wide strip. Referring to Adding the Borders on page 110, measure quilt through center from side to side. Cut two 2½"-wide strips to that measurement. Sew to top and bottom of quilt. Press seams toward border.

2. Measure quilt through center from top to bottom including borders just added. Cut two 2½"-wide strips to that measurement. Sew to sides of quilt. Press toward border.

3. Repeat steps 1 and 2 to join, measure, trim, and sew 1¾"-wide Second Border and 7½"-wide Outside Border strips to top, bottom, and sides of quilt. Press seams toward border.

layering & binding

1. Cut backing crosswise into two equal pieces and sew pieces together to make one 80" x 103" (approximate) backing piece. Press. Arrange and baste backing, batting, and top together, referring to Layering the Quilt on page 110.

2. Hand or machine quilt as desired. Or refer to photo on page 76 and the Big Stitch Quilting Technique on page 110. This quilt has a combination of machine and hand quilting. Seams were stitched in the ditch by machine, and then large background blocks were hand quilted with Big Stitch Quilting in a large "X". Refer to photo to arrange and sew assorted buttons to quilt.

3. Sew the 2¾" x 42" binding strips end-to-end to make one continuous 2¾"-wide binding strip. Refer to Binding the Quilt on page 111 and bind quilt to finish.

make it even easier

making the star gazer quilt reversible

To make the Quick and Cozy Bed Quilt a reversible backing for the Star Gazer Quilt, the back needs to be larger than the quilt top.

Fabric A (Dark) - 3¼ yards
    Four 26½" x 29½" pieces
Fabric B (Dark) - 1⅔ yards
    Two 26½" x 29½" pieces
Fabric C (Light) - 3¼ yards
    Four 26½" x 29½" pieces
Fabric D (Light) - 1⅔ yards
    Two 26½" x 29½" pieces

assembly

1. Sew one 26½" x 29½" Fabric D piece between two 26½" x 29½" Fabric A pieces. Press toward Fabric A. Make two.
2. Sew one 26½" x 29½" Fabric B piece between two 26½" x 29½" Fabric C pieces. Press toward Fabric B. Make two.
3. Arrange and sew alternating rows from steps 1 and 2 together to make quilt backing. Press.
4. Layer pieced backing (wrong side up), batting, and Star Gazer quilt top. Baste backing, batting, and top together referring to Layering the Quilt on page 110. Hand or machine quilt as desired.
5. Refer to Layering and Binding above and bind quilt to finish.

You'll never get tired of this quilt when there are two sides from which to choose. A simple large block arrangement gives a quick switch option.

camp kid
headboard

Finished size: 48" x 56"

No need to pitch a tent in the backyard when he can camp in his own room with this unique headboard! A simple wooden frame and easy fabric panels make this tent a cinch to construct.

fabric requirements & cutting instructions

Read all instructions before beginning and use ¼"-wide seam allowances throughout.

Camp Kid Headboard (Twin size)
MATERIALS NEEDED
Fabric A (Tent) - 3⅛ yards
Fabric B (Tent Flaps) - 3⅛ yards*
Fabric C (Tent Interior) - 1⅓ yards
Batting - Two 34" x 54" pieces
¼"-Thick Foam Board - 48" x 56"
Gold Yarn or Perle Cotton
Webbing and Rick Rack Trim - 1½ yards each
1" x 4" Lumber - Four 5-foot boards
1¼" Nails or Wood Screws
Staple Gun and Staples or Upholstery Tacks and Hammer
Metal Brace
Ruler with 30° angle mark
*Remaining fabric can be used for Quick & Cozy Pillow on page 80.

making the frame

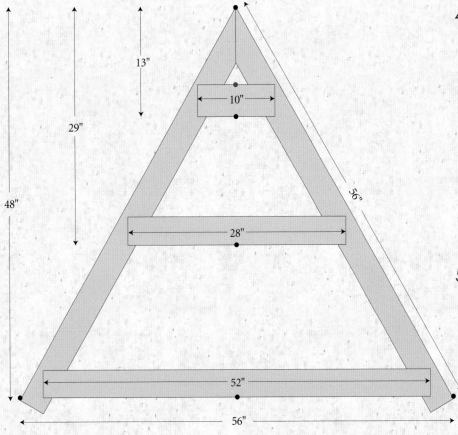

Frame Layout

1. Align ruler along the 30° mark to draw a cutting line on wood as shown. Cut on drawn line.

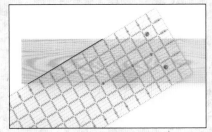

2. Referring to Frame Layout, measure 56" from the angle point, mark wood, and cut a straight line as shown in frame layout. Make two. From remaining wood, cut 10", 28" and 52" lengths.

3. If making the Camp Kid Flag (page 86), mark the top edge of 10" board at center point as indicated by red dot. Drill a 1½" deep hole in top edge to accommodate dowel.

4. Referring to Frame Layout, align the angled boards and attach a metal brace with either nails or screws. Please note, the brace used on our project was an item we had on hand; purchased braces may look different.

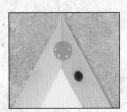

5. Arrange boards as shown in Frame Layout and nail or screw in place. This will be the back of frame.

companion project

finished size: 9½" x 15½"

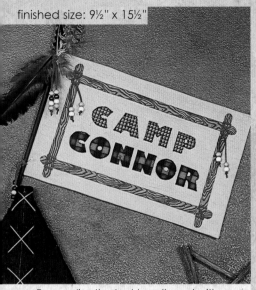

Personalize the tent headboard with his very own flag. Embellished with beads and leather, this fun flag will fly proudly over his tent!

camp kid flag

Fabric A (Flag Background) - ⅓ yard
   One 10" x 16" piece
Fabric B (Wood Border) - Scrap
   16" x 3" piece
Fabric C (Appliqué Letters) - Scraps
Backing - ⅜ yard
Batting-14" x 20"
Lightweight Fusible Web - ¾ yard
Leather Lacing - 1½ yards
Blue acrylic paint
Matte spray varnish
Assorted beads and feathers
⅜ " Dowel

making the flag

The instructions given are for quick-fuse appliqué. If you prefer traditional hand appliqué, add ¼" seam allowance when cutting appliqué pieces and refer to Hand Appliqué on page 109.

1. Refer to Quick-Fuse Appliqué on page 109. Fuse web to 16" x 3" Fabric B strip. Cut two ½" x 13½" and two ½" x 8¾" strips. Trim ends to round corners. Refer to photo to position and fuse appliqués to 10" x 16" Fabric A piece.

2. Choose lettering by selecting a font from the computer, a clip art alphabet book, or by drawing the letters. Adjust size of lettering to fit in center area of flag. Reverse all letters for quick-fuse appliqué. Fuse and cut letters from Fabric C for camp name. Arrange and fuse appliqué letters to flag. Finish all edges with machine zig zag stitch or decorative stitching as desired.

3. Layer backing and flag top, right sides together, on batting. Stitch around edges, using a ¼"-wide seam allowance and leave a 6" opening for turning. Trim batting and backing, clip corners, turn, and press. Hand stitch opening closed.

4. Machine or hand quilt as desired.

5. Referring to photo, sew 6" strips of leather lacing at border intersections. Attach beads as desired.

6. Mark center of two 12" leather lacings strips. Referring to photo, sew lacing to flag.

7. Determine height of flag pole and cut dowel to this measurement. Paint dowel with two coats of acrylic paint. Dry thoroughly and spray with several coats of matte spray varnish, following manufacturer's directions.

8. Tie flag to pole with leather lacing and attach beads and feathers as desired. Insert pole into previously drilled hole in headboard frame.

making the tent

1. Cut a piece of foam board at least 1" wider than inside measurements of frame, covering bottom board as shown.

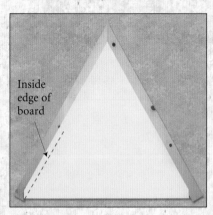

Inside edge of board

2. Cut sides of Fabric C 1½" larger on each side than foam board. Wrap bottom and sides of fabric to back of foam board and fasten with tape or glue. Note that top of foam board is not completely covered.

3. Arrange and nail foam board to front of frame as shown.

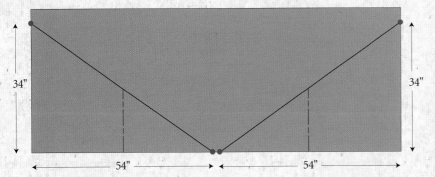

4. Cut Fabric A as shown, the large piece remaining can be used to cover back of frame, if desired. Follow same procedure to cut Fabric B.

34"   34"

54"   54"

5. Refer to photo on page 84 and red placement lines above to arrange and sew trim to Fabric A pieces as desired.

6. Layer one Fabric A and B piece, right sides together, on batting. Stitch along the 54" and 34" sides. Trim batting, clip corner, turn, and press. Use a zig zag to stitch diagonal side closed. Repeat for remaining pieces. The two completed units are mirror images..

7. Lay tent pieces from step 6 on frame. Referring to photo on page 84, determine desired flap opening and pin in place.

8. Referring to photo on page 84 and Embroidery Stitch Guide on page 110, use a Blind Stitch to sew sections together from top of tent to within 1" of flap opening. Remove tent from frame and embellish with yarn or perle cotton using a Cross Stitch design.

9. Wrap tent around frame, taping all sides temporarily in place. Staple or tack tent to back of frame, checking the front periodically to make sure fabric is smooth.

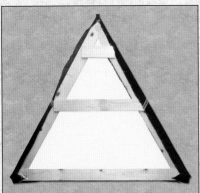

10. If desired, cover back with remaining Fabric A using upholstery tacks to secure in place and attach to wall or bed.

companion project

laced logs
bulletin board

Framed bulletin board
Four tree branches
Leather Lacing - 8 yards
Three 1" wood screws
Decorative beads

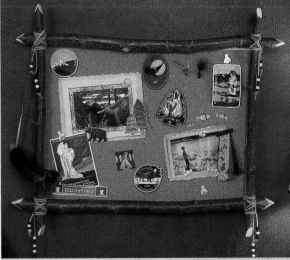

Complete your kid camp with a rustic bulletin board just right for displaying pictures, scouting badges, and small treasures.

making the bulletin board

1. Measure length and width of bulletin board frame. Ours measured 18" x 24". Cut two branches the length of the frame plus 4"-6". Cut two branches the width of the frame plus 4"-6".

2. Position the branches over the frame. Trim the underside of top and bottom branches to fit flat on the frame. Referring to photo above, trim both ends of each branch in an inverted "V". Using a chisel or saw, carefully notch the top and bottom branches as shown, so side pieces will fit more snugly.

3. With leather lacing, lash branches together. Allow excess length for decorative beads. Crisscross lacing on top of branch and wrap lacing around intersecting branch and tie. Thread beads as desired on lacing and tie a knot on each end. Repeat for all four corners.

4. Drill two ⅛"-wide holes through top of bulletin board frame and one hole in bottom. Place laced branches right side down on a sturdy work surface. Place bulletin board on logs. Check positioning. Insert wood screws into pre-drilled holes and screw through frame into branch. Add additional screws if needed.

trail map
night stand

What better way to remember favorite hikes and remote campsites than with a map-covered bedside table? Every time he looks at this table, those special outings will be vividly recalled.

Trail Map Nightstand
MATERIALS NEEDED

Purchased bedside table
Hiking Trail maps
Decoupage medium
Foam brushes
Burnt Umber Acrylic Paint - optional

getting started

Our nightstand is actually a computer printer stand that was purchased at a national discount department store. It was selected because of the large drawer and existing finish that complemented the map colors.

Our maps are from an old state road and recreation atlas that features landscape maps detailing mountains, rivers, and streams and shows hiking trails using red dots. Portions of eight different atlas pages were used on the top and six were used for the drawer.

embellishing the table

1. Decoupage medium was used to affix portions of the map to the tabletop and drawer. To get soft edges, selected portions were ripped from the maps. A variety of sizes can be used and for best effect, edges should be rounded and irregular. From the maps, select your favorite sites. Rip out an area, rounding edges.

2. Continue preparing pieces in the same manner, laying them on top of tabletop or drawer, overlapping edges, until the design desired is achieved. Allow enough extra to completely encase the edges.

3. When satisfied with the design, coat each piece with decoupage and apply to the tabletop or drawer, following the decoupage manufacturer's directions. After all map pieces have been applied, allow to dry thoroughly before adding two or more coats of decoupage medium to tabletop and drawer. Decoupage mediums vary, so carefully follow manufacturer's directions. If an antiqued finish is desired, mix a small amount of burnt umber acrylic paint with decoupage medium for a final coat. Experiment before applying.

4. When decoupage application is complete and thoroughly dry, add drawer pull and accessorize with camping gear and books.

tip

A lantern is the perfect night light when sleeping under the stars in this camp-themed bedroom. An inexpensive garden candle lantern is easily converted into an electric night light by drilling a hole in the lantern bottom and inserting a purchased electrical component. Use a low wattage electrical cord and socket component (sold as an accessory for lighted ceramic houses).

After drilling, make sure that any sharp edges are covered with electrical tape before inserting the light into the lantern. The electrical component includes a metal collar to hold the light in place, or use electrical tape to hold component in place.

For more starlight ambiance, apply spots of glow-in-the-dark paint to the room ceiling for a twinkly surprise for nightly campouts.

tropical paradise

Transport your family to a tropical paradise brimming with vibrant colors, lush flowers, and swaying palms. From the colorplay pillows, to the hibiscus lap quilt, to the tropical palms on the wall, you'll want to sink your feet into the sands of creative quilting with these projects for inspiration!

exotic flower
lap quilt

Finished size: 58½" x 61"
Vibrant colors and a pieced hibiscus design make this quilt the epitome of the tropics!
Four large blocks are easily constructed and embellished with dimensional purple accents. For an
even faster introduction to the tropics, make one block for a striking wall quilt or oversized pillow.

fabric requirements & cutting instructions

Read all instructions before beginning and use ¼"-wide seam allowances throughout. Read Cutting the Strips and Pieces on page 108 prior to cutting fabrics.

Exotic Flower Lap Quilt 58½" x 61"	FIRST CUT		SECOND CUT	
	Number of Strips or Pieces	Dimensions	Number of Pieces	Dimensions
Fabric A Background 1⅝ yards	2	7½" x 42"	8	7½" squares
	4	3½" x 42"	8	3½" x 8½"
			16	3½" squares
	3	2½" x 42"	4	2½" x 5½"
			8	2½" x 3½"
			16	2½" squares
	6	2" x 42"	8	1½" x 4½"
	2	1½" x 42"	8	1½" squares
Fabric B Light Petals ⅔ yard	3	6½" x 42"	4	6½" x 11½"
			4	6½" x 8½"
	1	1½" x 42"	4	1½" x 3½"
			12	1½" squares
Fabric C Medium Petals ⅜ yard	1	4½" x 42"	4	4½" x 6½"
	1	3½" x 42"	4	3½" x 5½"
	1	2½" x 42"	4	2½" x 3½"
			8	2½" squares
Fabric D Dark Petals ⅝ yard	1	6½" x 42"	4	6½" x 8½"
	1	4½" x 42"	4	4½" x 6½"
	1	3½" x 42"	4	3½" x 5½"
	1	2½" x 42"	4	2½" x 3½"
			8	2½" squares
	1	1½" x 42"	4	1½" x 3½"
			12	1½" squares
Fabric E Flower Center ⅛ yard	1	2½" x 42"	4	2½" x 3½"

BORDERS

First Border ¼ yard	5	1" x 42"		
Second Border ⅓ yard	5	2" x 42"		
Outside Border 1 yard	6	5" x 42"		
Binding ⅝ yard	6	2¾" x 42"		

Flower Pistils - ½ yard
Backing - 3⅔ yards
Batting - 65" x 67"

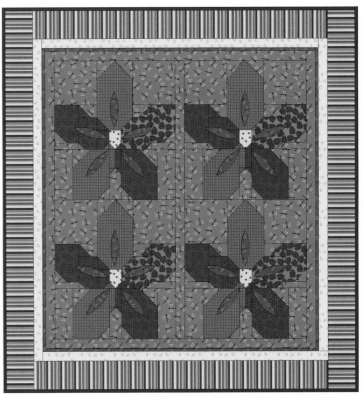

exotic flower lap quilt
finished size: 58½" x 61"
photo: opposite page

getting started

You will be making four Exotic Flower Blocks. Blocks measure 20½" x 22½" unfinished. Refer to Accurate Seam Allowance on page 108 before making blocks. Use the Assembly Line Method on page 108 whenever possible. Press seams in direction of arrows.

making the exotic flower blocks

1. Refer to Quick Corner Triangles on page 108. Sew 2½" Fabric A square to 4½" x 6½" Fabric D piece as shown. Press. Make four. Sew 2½" Fabric A square to 4½" x 6½" Fabric C piece. Press. Make four.

A = 2½ x 2½
D = 4½ x 6½
Make 4

A = 2½ x 2½
C = 4½ x 6½
Make 4

2. Sew 1½" x 4½" Fabric A piece to unit from step 1 as shown. Press. Make eight, four of each variation.

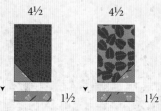

Make 8
(4 of each variation)

3. Making quick corner triangle units, sew 2½" Fabric D square to 2½" x 3½" Fabric A piece, as shown. Press. Make four. Sew 2½" Fabric C square to 2½" x 3½" Fabric A piece. Press. Make four.

D = 2½ x 2½
A = 2½ x 3½
Make 4

C = 2½ x 2½
A = 2½ x 3½
Make 4

4. Making quick corner triangle units, sew 1½" Fabric A square to 3½" x 5½" Fabric D piece, as shown. Press. Make four. Sew 1½" Fabric A square to 3½" x 5½" Fabric C piece. Press. Make four.

A = 1½ x 1½
D = 3½ x 5½
Make 4

A = 1½ x 1½
C = 3½ x 5½
Make 4

5. Matching fabrics, sew unit from step 3 to unit from step 4 as shown. Press. Make eight, four of each variation.

Make 8
(4 of each variation)

6. Sew unit from step 2 to unit from step 5, matching fabrics as shown. Press. Make eight, four of each variation.

Make 8
(4 of each variation)

7. Sew 7½" Fabric A square to unit from step 6 as shown. Press. Make eight, four of each variation.

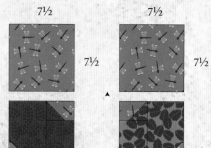

Make 8
(4 of each variation)

8. Making quick corner triangle units, sew two 3½" Fabric A squares, one 2½" Fabric D square and one 2½" Fabric C square to 6½" x 11½" Fabric B piece as shown. Press. Make four.

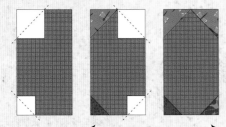

A = 3½ x 3½
D = 2½ x 2½
C = 2½ x 2½
B = 6½ x 11½
Make 4

9. Making quick corner triangle units, sew 1½" Fabric B square to 2½" x 3½" Fabric D piece, as shown. Press. Make four. Sew 1½" Fabric D square to 2½" x 3½" Fabric C piece, as shown. Press. Make four.

B = 1½ x 1½
D = 2½ x 3½
Make 4

D = 1½ x 1½
C = 2½ x 3½
Make 4

10. Making quick corner triangle units, sew one 1½" Fabric B and one 1½" Fabric D square to 2½" x 3½" Fabric E piece, as shown. Press. Make four.

B = 1½ x 1½
D = 1½ x 1½
E = 2½ x 3½
Make 4

11. Sew unit from step 10 between one of each unit from step 9, matching triangle corners as shown. Press. Make four.

Make 4

12. Sew unit from step 8 to unit from step 11 as shown. Press. Make four.

Make 4

13. Sew unit from step 12 between two units, one of each variation, from step 7 as shown. Press. Make four.

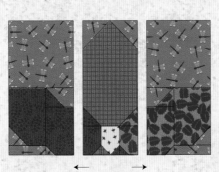

Make 4

14. Making quick corner triangle units, sew one 3½" and one 2½" Fabric A square to 6½" x 8½" Fabric B piece as shown. Press. Make four. Sew one 2½" and one 3½" Fabric A square to 6½" x 8½" Fabric D piece as shown. Press. Make four.

A = 3½ x 3½
    2½ x 2½
B = 6½ x 8½
Make 4

A = 2½ x 2½
    3½ x 3½
D = 6½ x 8½
Make 4

15. Sew 3½" x 8½" Fabric A piece to each unit from step 14 as shown. Press. Make eight, four of each variation.

3½

8½

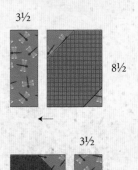

3½

8½

Make 8
(4 of each variation)

16. Making quick corner triangle units, sew one 1½" Fabric B and one 1½" Fabric D square to 2½" x 5½" Fabric A piece as shown. Press. Make four.

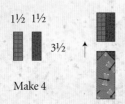

B = 1½ x 1½
D= 1½ x 1½
A = 2½ x 5½
Make 4

17. Sew 1½" x 3½" Fabric B and 1½" x 3½" Fabric D pieces together as shown. Press seam open. Matching fabrics, sew to unit from step 16. Press. Make four.

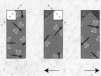

1½ 1½

3½

Make 4

Make 4

18. Sew unit from step 17 between two units, one of each variation, from step 15 as shown. Press. Make four.

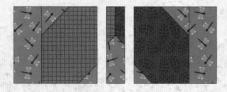

Make 4

19. Sew unit from step 13 to unit from step 18 as shown. Press. Make four. Block measures 20½" x 22½".

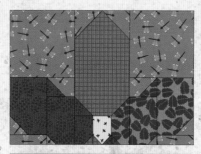

Make 4
Block measures 20½" x 22½"

assembling the quilt

1. Referring to photo and layout on pages 92 and 93, sew blocks together in vertical pairs. Press.

2. Sew 2" x 42" Fabric A strips together end-to-end to make one continuous 2"-wide strip. Measure through center of block pairs from top to bottom. Cut one strip to this length and sew between vertical rows. Press.

3. Referring to Adding the Borders on page 110, measure quilt through center from side to side. Cut two 2"-wide Fabric A strips to this length. Sew to top and bottom of quilt. Press seams toward border.

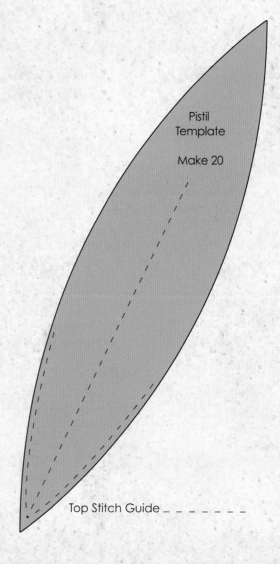

Pistil
Template

Make 20

Top Stitch Guide _ _ _ _ _ _ _

4. Measure quilt through center from top to bottom, including the borders just added. Cut two 2"-wide Fabric A strips to this length. Sew to sides of quilt. Press toward border.

5. Repeat steps 3 and 4 to join, measure, trim, and sew 1"-wide First Border, 2"-wide Second Border, and 5"-wide Outside Border to top, bottom, and sides of quilt. Press seams toward borders.

layering & binding

1. Cut backing into two equal pieces. Sew pieces together to make one 65" x 80" (approximate) backing piece. Press. Trim backing to 65" x 67". Arrange and baste backing, batting, and top together, referring to Layering the Quilt on page 110.

2. Hand or machine quilt as desired.

3. Sew 2¾" x 42" binding strips end-to-end to make one continuous 2¾"-wide binding strip. Press. Refer to Binding the Quilt on page 111 and bind quilt to finish.

adding the embellishment

1. Refer to Pistil Template on page 96. Trace twenty Pistils on the wrong side of fabric. Place traced fabric right sides together, on top of a matching-size piece of fabric and batting. Stitch on drawn line.

2. Trim batting close to stitching. Cut out pistil, leaving ¼"-wide seam allowance. Clip curves. Slit the back of one piece of fabric and turn right side out. Press. Make twenty.

3. Refer to photo and layout on pages 92 and 93 and Pistil Template on page 96. Position pistils and top stitch to quilt as indicated on template.

make it even easier

exotic flower wall quilt

Finished size: 28" x 39"

The Exotic Flower Lap Quilt on page 92 consists of four flower blocks. The wall quilt has only one flower block. For Fabrics A through E, refer to chart below for yardage and fabric chart on page 93 for cuts. Divide the number of pieces under Second Cut by four to make one block. Additional cuts are listed below.

Fabric A (Background) - ⅔ yard
  Two 2" x 25½" strips
  Two 2" x 20½" strips
Fabric B (Light Petals) - ¼ yard
Fabric C (Medium Petals) - ¼ yard
Fabric D (Dark Petals) - ¼ yard
Fabric E (Flower Center) - Scrap

First Border - ⅙ yard
  Two 1" x 26½" strips
  Two 1" x 23½" strips
Second Border - ⅓ yard
  Two 2" x 29½" strips
  Two 2" x 24½" strips
Outside Border - ⅓ yard
  Two 5" x 27½" strips
Binding - ⅜ yard
  Four 2¾" x 42" strips
Flower Pistils - ¼ yard
Backing - 1 yard (43" wide or wider)
Batting - 32" x 43"

getting started

You will be making one Exotic Flower Block. Refer to Exotic Flower Lap Quilt, steps 1-19, pages 94-96.

making the wall quilt

1. Sew two 2" x 20½" Fabric A strips to top and bottom of Exotic Flower Block. Press toward border. Sew two 2" x 25½" Fabric A strips to sides. Press.

2. Sew unit from step 1 between two 1" x 23½" First Border strips. Press toward border. Sew this unit between two 1" x 26½" First Border strips. Press.

3. Sew unit from step 2 between two 2" x 24½" Second Border strips. Press toward border just sewn. Sew unit between two 2" x 29½" Second Border strips. Press.

4. Sew two 5" x 27½" Outside Border strips to top and bottom of quilt. Press.

5. Arrange and baste backing, batting, and top together, referring to Layering the Quilt on page 110. Hand or machine quilt as desired.

6. Refer to Binding the Quilt on page 111 and bind quilt to finish.

7. Refer to Adding the Embellishment at top of page, steps 1-3, to add five pistil pieces to quilt.

Like a flower behind the ear, add a playful punch of tropical color by making one Exotic Flower block into a simple, yet stunning, wallhanging.

tropical palm
wall quilt

Finished size: 33" x 43"
You can almost feel the warm breeze blowing and the hot sand on your feet
with this Tropical Palm Wall Quilt. Set the scene for your own tropical paradise with easy
dimensional flowers, frayed-edge leaves, and a hula skirt-style fringe!

fabric requirements & cutting instructions

Read all instructions before beginning and use
¼"-wide seam allowances throughout. Read Cutting the
Strips and Pieces on page 108 prior to cutting fabrics.

Tropical Palm Wall Quilt 33" x 43"	FIRST CUT	
	Number of Strips or Pieces	Dimensions
Fabric A Sky ¾ yard	1	22½" x 23½"
Fabric B Dark Sea ⅛ yard	1	1½" x 23½"
Fabric C Light Sea ¾ yard* (directional) *OR* ⅙ yard (non-directional)	1	23½" x 3½"
Fabric D Sand ⅙ yard	1 1 1 1	3½" x 11" 3½" square 2" x 7" 2" square
Fabric E Grass ¼ yard	1 1 1	4½" x 23½" 3½" x 6½" 2" x 7"
BORDERS		
First Border ⅙ yard	3	1" x 42"
Outside Border ⅝ yard	4	4½" x 42"
Binding ⅜ yard	4	2¾" x 42"

Tree Trunks - ½ yard or one fat quarter for
   tall trees, and ⅓ yard or one obese eighth for
   short tree
Leaf and Flower Appliqués - Assorted scraps
Backing - 1⅓ yards
Batting - 37" x 47"
4" Beaded Fringe - 1 yard
Chenille Trim - 1 yard
Assorted Ribbons - 6" scraps
Template Plastic
#5 Perle Cotton - Two shades of green
** For directional fabric the measurement that is listed
first runs parallel to selvage (strip width).*

tropical palm wall quilt
finished size: 33" x 43"
photo: opposite page

getting started

This wall quilt is fast to piece. Most of the details are added after quilting. For a touch of fun, we added a beaded fringe. Press seams in direction of arrows.

making the background

1. Sew 1½" x 23½" Fabric B strip between 22½" x 23½" Fabric A piece and 23½" x 3½" Fabric C strip as shown. Press.

23½

22½

1½

3½

2. Refer to Quick Corner Triangles on page 108. Sew 3½" Fabric D square to 3½" x 6½" Fabric E piece as shown. Press.

D = 3½ x 3½
E = 3½ x 6½

3. Making a quick corner triangle unit, sew 2" Fabric D square to 2" x 7" Fabric E piece as shown. Press.

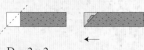

D = 2 x 2
E = 2 x 7

4. Sew 2" x 7" Fabric D piece to unit from step 3 as shown. Press.

7

2

5. Sew 3½" x 11" Fabric D piece between units from step 2 and step 4 as shown. Press.

11

3½

6. Sew unit from step 5 between unit from step 1 and 4½" x 23½" Fabric E piece shown. Press.

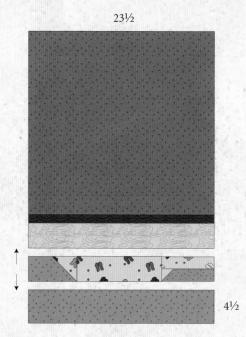

23½

4½

adding the borders

1. Sew 1" x 42" First Border strips together end-to-end to make one continuous 1"-wide strip. Refer to Adding the Borders on page 110. Measure quilt through center from side to side. Cut two 1"-wide strips to that measurement. Sew to top and bottom of quilt. Press seams toward border.

2. Measure quilt through center from top to bottom including the borders just added. Cut two 1"-wide First Border strips to that measurement. Sew to sides of quilt. Press.

3. Repeat steps 1 and 2 to join, measure, trim, and sew 4½"-wide Outside Border strips to top, bottom, and sides of quilt. Press.

adding the tree trunks

1. From tall tree-trunk fabric, cut two 2¾"-wide bias strips as shown. From short tree-trunk fabric, cut one 2¾"-wide bias strip.

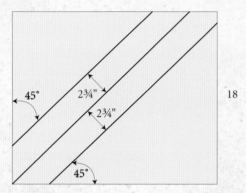

18

2. Referring to photo and layout on pages 98 and 99, arrange bias strips for tree trunks on quilt top, turning edges of bias strips under so that tree trunks measure approximately 1¾"-wide at base and 1"-wide at top of trees. Press. Tree trunks are approximately 22", 20", and 14"-tall finished. Machine or hand-stitch edges in place.

hula lamp

Purchased "bamboo" lamp
Lined fabric lampshade
Beaded fringe
Tan paint
Paintbrush
Dark brown antiquing medium
Matte spray varnish

This stylish lamp will hula into your heart with its swaying beads and "bamboo" base. A purchased lamp and shade can be easily painted and embellished for this popular home decorating theme.

making the lamp

1. Sand lamp to remove any oils or finish. Use tack cloth or damp rag to remove residue. Paint with tan paint. Allow to dry.

2. Following manufacturer's directions, apply antiquing medium to lamp. Allow heavier coverage in recesses of lamp.

3. When antiquing is dry, spray matte varnish on lamp following manufacturer's directions.

4. Referring to photo, pin fabric tape of beaded fringe to lining at top of lampshade, overlapping ends of fabric tape ½". Making sure tape is well hidden, use an overcast stitch to stitch top and bottom edges of tape to lining of shade.

5. Carefully turn lampshade upside down. Referring to step 4, pin fabric tape of beaded fringe to lining of lampshade bottom. Hand-stitch in place.

layering & binding

1. Cut backing to 37" x 47". Arrange and baste backing, batting, and top together, referring to Layering the Quilt on page 110.

2. Hand or machine quilt as desired.

3. Sew 2¾" x 42" binding strips end-to-end to make one continuous 2¾"-wide binding strip. Press. Refer to Binding the Quilt on page 111 and bind quilt to finish.

adding the embellishments

1. Trace Palm Leaf Appliqué Templates on page 103 onto template plastic. Use assorted scraps to trace and cut eighteen of Palm Leaf A, twenty-four of Palm Leaf B, and fifteen of Palm Leaf C. Place matching size palm leaves together in layers of three, with right sides up. Stitch around each set, ⅜" from edge. Clip ¼" apart and ¼" deep to fringe palm-leaf sets as shown. Wet leaf sets with cold water and towel dry. Place leaves and towel in dryer. Dry on hot setting to fluff leaves.

2. Referring to photo and layout on pages 98 and 99, arrange palm leaf sets on quilt. Stitch leaves to quilt with single or double line of stitching as desired.

3. Referring to photo and layout on pages 98 and 99, position and pin chenille trim in a spiral on quilt top. Stitch chenille trim to quilt top starting at center of sun and stitching along center of strip.

4. For flowers, trace four 3½" and three 3" circles onto wrong side of assorted scraps using the templates at left. Place traced fabric right sides together with matching size scrap and stitch along traced line. Cut out circles, leaving ³⁄₁₆" seam allowance. On back of circle, make small slit for turning. Clip around seam allowance, turn and press.

5. For each flower, fold 6"-length of ribbon in center to form a loop. With ends of ribbon, make a shorter loop on each side of center fold. Stitch to secure.

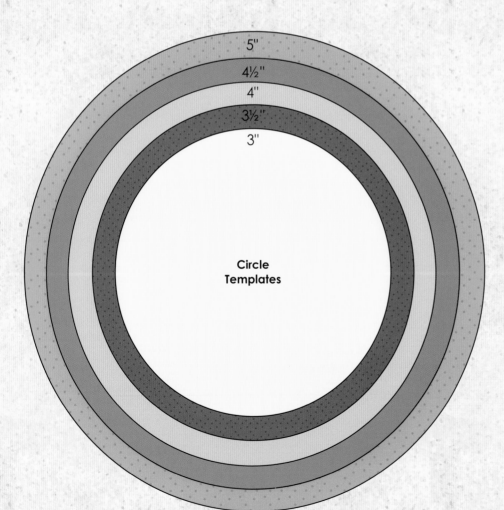

5"
4½"
4"
3½"
3"

Circle Templates

tropical accent pillows

Fabric A (Pillow Center) - ⅜ yard
  One 11½" square
Fabric B (Border and Backing) - ½ yard
  Two 2" x 14½" strips
  Two 2" x 11½" strips
  Two 10" x 14½" pieces
Fabric C (Small Flower) - Scrap
  Two 4" pieces
Fabric D (Large Flower) - Scrap
  Two 5" pieces
Decorative Trim - 1" beaded fringe
Lining and Batting - 16½" square of each
Pillow Form - 14" square

finished size: 14" square

Add to the tropical ambiance with simple small pillows that mix and match beautifully with the Hot Tropics Colorplay Pillows (page 104)– especially when embellished with dimensional flowers and bead centers!

6. At center of large circles, run a line of basting stitches 1¼" in diameter as shown. Pull thread slightly to gather, insert ribbon from step 5, and tie off. Stitch to secure ribbon. Repeat with small circles, running basting stitches 1" in diameter. Referring to photo on page 98, tack flowers to quilt.

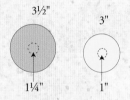

3½"

3"

1¼"

1"

Basting Stitches

7. For grass, cut a 2" x 4" piece of cardboard. Cut a ⅛"-wide slot as shown. Wrap both colors of perle cotton strands around cardboard. Vary the number of wraps for each set of grass. With small stitches, sew through the middle of perle cotton in the slot, making sure all pieces have been sewn. Cut the folded edges of strands along cardboard edges.

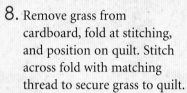

8. Remove grass from cardboard, fold at stitching, and position on quilt. Stitch across fold with matching thread to secure grass to quilt.

9. Sew 4" beaded fringe to bottom of quilt.

making the pillows

1. Sew 11½" Fabric A square between two 2" x 11½" Fabric B strips. Press. Sew 2" x 14½" Fabric B strips to remaining sides. Press.

2. Refer to Finishing Pillows on page 111 to quilt pillow top and sew backing piece to pillow.

3. Trace 3½" circle on page 102 on wrong side of Fabric C. Place traced fabric right sides together with a matching piece of fabric. Sew on traced line. Trim fabric, leaving ⅜" seam allowance. Clip curves. Make a small slit in one circle and turn right side out. Press. Baste a 1" circle in center of circle. Draw up basting threads to gather circle. Insert tape of beaded fringe in center of small circle and stitch in place, covering tape.

4. Repeat step 3 tracing a 4½" circle on Fabric D to make a large flower. Baste a 1¼" circle in center of flower instead of 1", and do not add beads. Insert flower from step 3 into center of 4½" flower. Draw up basting threads of 1¼" circle to enclose center of smaller flower, and stitch flowers together. Referring to photograph, stitch flowers to center of pillow top, being careful to avoid stitching through backing. Insert a 14" pillow form or refer to Pillow Forms on page 111.

Palm Leaf Templates

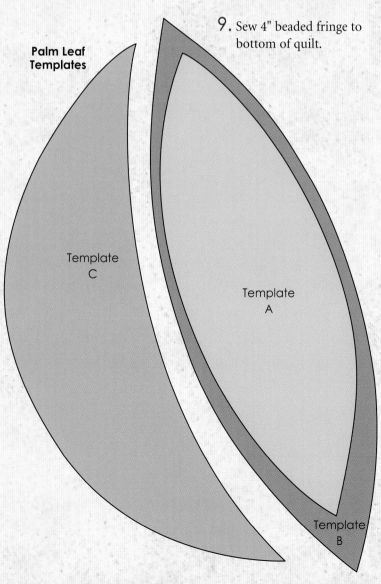

Template C

Template A

Template B

hot tropics
colorplay pillows

Finished size: 20½" square
Have fun with hot colors when you make these easygoing home dec pillows.
Tropical insects are embroidered in the centers, but these would be just as appealing with
plain or "fussy cut" centers. Combine a variety of colors for a sunny sensation.

fabric requirements & cutting instructions

Read all instructions before beginning and use ¼"-wide seam allowances throughout. Read Cutting the Strips and Pieces on page 108 prior to cutting fabrics.

Hot Tropics Colorplay Pillow A 20½" square Makes one pillow	FIRST CUT		SECOND CUT	
	Number of Strips or Pieces	Dimensions	Number of Pieces	Dimensions
Fabric A Scrap	1	4" square*		
Fabric B ⅓ yard	3	2½" x 42"	2 2 2 2	2½" x 21" 2½" x 17" 2½" x 8" 2½" x 4"
Fabric C ⅛ yard	1	1½" x 42"	2 2	1½" x 10" 1½" x 8"
Fabric D ⅙ yard	2	1½" x 42"	2 2	1½" x 12" 1½" x 10"
Fabric E ⅙ yard	2	2" x 42"	2 2	2" x 15" 2" x 12"
Fabric F ⅙ yard	2	1½" x 42"	2 2	1½" x 17" 1½" x 15"
Backing ⅔ yard	2	13" x 21"		

Lining - ⅔ yard
Batting - 24" square
Pillow Form - 20½"

*If you choose to machine embroider the center, we recommend starting with an 8" square and then trimming to 4" square after embroidering.

Hot Tropics Colorplay Pillow B 20½" square Makes one pillow	FIRST CUT		SECOND CUT	
	Number of Strips or Pieces	Dimensions	Number of Pieces	Dimensions
Fabric A ¼ yard	2	2½" x 42"	2 2	2½" x 21" 2½" x 17"
Fabric B ¼ yard	1 2	4" square* 2½" x 42"	2 2	2½" x 17" 2½" x 13"
Fabric C ⅙ yard	2	1½" x 42"	2 2	1½" x 13" 1½" x 11"
Fabric D ⅛ yard	1	1½" x 42"	2 2	1½" x 11" 1½" x 9"
Fabric E ⅛ yard	1	2" x 42"	2 2	2" x 9" 2" x 6"
Fabric F ⅛ yard	1	1½" x 42"	2 2	1½" x 6" 1½" x 4"
Backing ⅔ yard	2	13" x 21"		

Lining - ⅔ yard
Batting - 24" square
Pillow Form - 20½"

*If you choose to machine embroider the center, we recommend starting with an 8" square and then trimming to 4" square after embroidering.

getting started

Pillow A is constructed by adding pairs of graduating strips. Pillow B is constructed in the same manner, reversing the order of colors. If desired, add embroidery to the center square or appliqué a design, such as the Butterfly Appliqué on page 12.

tip *The design on the 4" center square on each pillow was made with the The Good Life by Debbie Mumm® embroidery card and a Bernina® artista 200E. The card is available from Bernina dealers or www.embroideryonline.com.*

making pillow A

1. Sew 4" Fabric A square between two 2½" x 4" Fabric B Pieces. Press. Sew this unit between two 2½" x 8" Fabric B pieces as shown. Press.

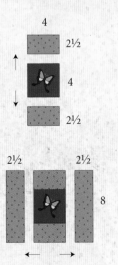

2. Sew unit from step 1 between two 1½" x 8" Fabric C pieces. Press. Sew this unit between two 1½" x 10" Fabric C pieces as shown. Press.

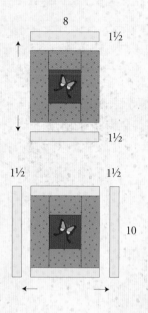

3. Sew unit from step 2 between two 1½" x 10" Fabric D pieces. Press. Sew this unit between two 1½" x 12" Fabric D pieces as shown. Press.

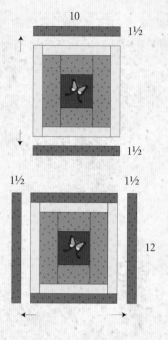

4. Sew unit from step 3 between two 2" x 12" Fabric E pieces. Press. Sew this unit between two 2" x 15" Fabric E pieces as shown. Press.

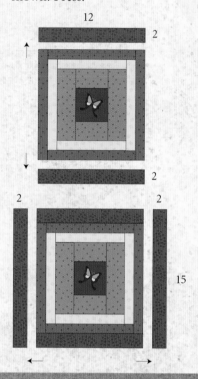

make it even easier

quick n' easy tropical pillows

Achieve the effect of the colorplay pillows without a lot of sewing by using striped fabric. Select 1⅓ yards* of fabric that has a horizontal repeat of at least two 12" sections. If the striped section does not have two repeats from selvage to selvage, you will need 2⅔ yards of fabric.

materials needed

Fabric A (Stripe) -
   1⅓* or 2⅔ yards
Backing - ⅔ yard
   Two 13" x 21" pieces
Batting and Lining - ¾ yard
   25" square of each
Pillow Form - 20½" square

instructions

1. Make a triangular paper pattern. The triangle should have a 22" base, and height of 11". Check the angles with your rotary ruler. The top angle will be 90° (corner of ruler) and the other two angles 45°.

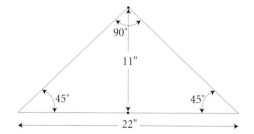

2. From the striped fabric, cut four identical triangles parallel to selvage of fabric as shown.

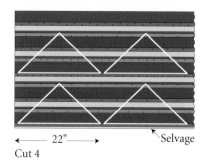

Cut 4

3. Using a ¼"-wide seam, sew the triangles together in pairs along one short side, matching stripes. Press. Then sew the pairs together along the long side to form a square pillow top. Press. Square the pillow top to 21". Embroider center of pillow, if desired.

4. Follow steps 1 and 2 under Hot Tropics Colorplay Pillows, Layering and Finishing, page 107, to finish pillow and make pillow form.

   You may have enough fabric left after cutting four triangles to make another pillow with the reverse pattern.

5. Sew unit from step 4 between two 1½" x 15" Fabric F pieces. Press. Sew this unit between two 1½" x 17" Fabric F pieces as shown. Press.

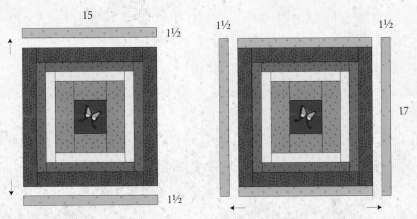

layering & finishing

1. Refer to Finishing Pillows on page 111, step 1, to quilt pillow top. To give the appearance of mitered corners, we used charcoal-colored thread to machine stitch diagonal lines across the pillow, but did not stitch through the embroidery. Remaining quilting was done with invisible thread.

2. Refer to page 111, Finishing Pillows, steps 2-4, to sew 13" x 21" backings to pillow, and to make pillow form, if desired.

6. Sew unit from step 5 between two 2½" x 17" Fabric B pieces. Press. Sew this unit between two 2½" x 21" Fabric B pieces. Press. Block measures 21" square.

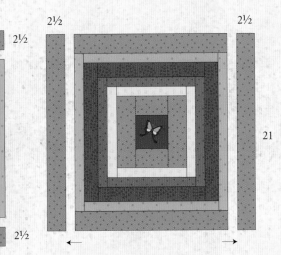

Block A measures 21" square

making pillow B

Beginning with 4" Fabric B square, repeat procedure used for Pillow A to assemble Pillow B, referring to diagram for piece dimensions and fabric placement. Press after adding each new piece. Block measures 21" square. Continue with Layering & Finishing above to complete the pillow.

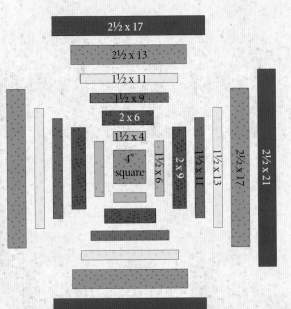

general directions

cutting the strips and pieces

Before you make each of the projects in this book, pre-wash and press the fabrics. Using a rotary cutter, see-through ruler, and a cutting mat, cut the strips and pieces for the project. If indicated on the Cutting Chart, some will need to be cut again into smaller strips and pieces. Make second cuts in order shown to maximize use of fabric. The approximate width of the fabric is 42". Measurements for all pieces include ¼"-wide seam allowance unless otherwise indicated. Press in the direction of the arrows.

fussy cut

To make a "fussy cut," carefully position ruler or template over a selected design in fabric. Include seam allowances before cutting desired pieces.

assembly line method

Whenever possible, use an assembly line method. Position pieces right sides together and line up next to sewing machine. Stitch first unit together, then continue sewing others without breaking threads. When all units are sewn, clip threads to separate. Press in direction of arrows.

accurate seam allowance

Accurate seam allowances are always important, but especially when the quilt top contains multiple pieced borders with lots of blocks and seams! If each seam is off as little as ¹⁄₁₆", you'll soon find yourself struggling with components that just won't fit.

To ensure you are stitching a perfect ¼"-wide seam, try this simple test: Cut three strips of fabric, each exactly 1½" x 12". With right sides together, and long raw edges aligned, sew two strips together, carefully maintaining a ¼" seam. Press. Add the third strip to complete the strip set. Press seams to one side and measure. The finished strip set should measure 3½" x 12". The center strip should measure 1"-wide, the two outside strips 1¼"-wide, and the seam allowances exactly ¼".

If your measurements differ, check to make sure that you have pressed the seams flat. If your strip set still doesn't "measure up," try stitching a new strip set, adjusting the seam allowance until you are able to achieve a perfect ¼"-wide seam.

quick corner triangles

Quick corner triangles are formed by simply sewing fabric squares to other squares or rectangles. The directions and diagrams with each project illustrate what size pieces to use and where to place squares on the corresponding piece. Follow steps 1–3 below to make quick corner triangle units.

1. With pencil and ruler, draw diagonal line on wrong side of fabric square that will form the triangle. See Diagram A. This will be your **sewing** line.

A.
sewing line

2. With right sides together, place square on corresponding piece. Matching raw edges, pin in place, and sew ON drawn line. Trim off excess fabric, leaving ¼" seam allowance as shown in Diagram B.

B.
trim ¼" away from sewing line

3. Press seam in direction of arrow as shown in step-by-step project diagram. Measure completed corner triangle unit to ensure the greatest accuracy.

C.
finished quick corner triangle unit

quick-fuse appliqué

Quick-fuse appliqué is a method of adhering appliqué pieces to a background with fusible web. For quick and easy results, simply quick-fuse appliqué pieces in place. Use sewable, lightweight fusible web for the projects in this book unless otherwise indicated. Finishing raw edges with stitching is desirable; laundering is not recommended unless edges are finished.

1. With paper side up, lay fusible web over appliqué design. Leaving ½" space between pieces, trace all elements of design. Cut around traced pieces, approximately ¼" outside traced line. See Diagram A.

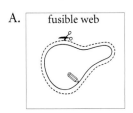
A. fusible web

2. With paper side up, position and iron fusible web to wrong side of selected fabrics. Follow manufacturer's directions for iron temperature and fusing time. Cut out each piece on traced line. See Diagram B.

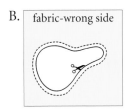
B. fabric-wrong side

3. Remove paper backing from pieces. A thin film will remain on wrong side of fabric. Position and fuse all pieces of one appliqué design at a time onto background, referring to photos for placement. Fused design will be the reverse of traced pattern.

appliqué pressing sheet

An appliqué pressing sheet is very helpful when there are many small elements to apply using a quick-fuse appliqué technique. The pressing sheet allows small items to be bonded together before applying them to the background. The sheet is coated with a special material that prevents the fusible web from adhering permanently to the sheet. Follow manufacturer's directions. Remember to let the fabric cool completely before lifting it from the appliqué sheet. If not cooled, the fusible web could remain on the sheet instead of on the fabric.

machine appliqué

This technique should be used when you are planning to launder quick-fuse projects. Several different stitches can be used: small narrow zig zag stitch, satin stitch, blanket stitch, or another decorative machine stitch. Use an open toe appliqué foot if your machine has one. Use a stabilizer to obtain even stitches and help prevent puckering. Always practice first to check machine settings.

1. Fuse all pieces following Quick-Fuse Appliqué directions.

2. Cut a piece of stabilizer large enough to extend beyond the area you are stitching. Pin to the wrong side of fabric.

3. Select thread to match appliqué.

4. Following the order that appliqués were positioned, stitch along the edges of each section. Anchor beginning and ending stitches by tying off or stitching in place two or three times.

5. Complete all stitching, then remove stabilizer.

hand appliqué

Hand appliqué is easy when you start out with the right supplies. Cotton or machine embroidery thread is easy to work with. Pick a color that matches the appliqué fabric as closely as possible. Use appliqué or silk pins for holding shapes in place and a long, thin needle, such as a sharp, for stitching.

1. Make a template for every shape in the appliqué design. Use a dotted line to show where pieces overlap.

2. Place template on right side of appliqué fabric. Trace around template.

3. Cut out shapes ¼" beyond traced line.

4. Position shapes on background fabric, referring to quilt layout. Pin shapes in place.

5. When layering and stitching appliqué shapes, always work from background to foreground. Where shapes overlap, do not turn under and stitch edges of bottom pieces. Turn and stitch the edges of the piece on top.

6. Use the traced line as your turn-under guide. Entering from the wrong side of the appliqué shape, bring the needle up on the traced line. Using the tip of the needle, turn under the fabric along the traced line. Using blind stitch, stitch along the folded edge to join the appliqué shape to the background fabric. Turn under and stitch about ¼" at a time.

adding the borders

1. Measure quilt through the center from side to side. Trim two border strips to this measurement. Sew to top and bottom of quilt. Press toward border.

2. Measure quilt through the center from top to bottom, including borders added in step 1. Trim border strips to this measurement. Sew to sides and press. Repeat to add additional borders.

layering the quilt

1. Cut backing and batting 4" to 8" larger than quilt top.

2. Lay pressed backing on bottom (right side down), batting in middle, and pressed quilt top (right side up) on top. Make sure everything is centered and that backing and batting are flat. Backing and batting will extend beyond quilt top.

3. Begin basting in center and work toward outside edges. Baste vertically and horizontally, forming a 3"–4" grid. Baste or pin completely around edge of quilt top. Quilt as desired. Remove basting.

big stitch quilting technique

If you plan to combine machine quilting and the Big Stitch Technique, complete machine quilting first. To make a Big Stitch, use embroidery needle with perle cotton, crochet thread, or embroidery floss. Anchor knot in the batting as in quilting. Make ¼"-long stitches on top of quilt and ⅛"-long stitches under quilt, so large stitches stand out.

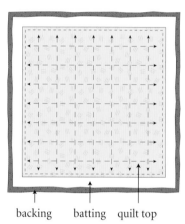

backing   batting   quilt top

embroidery stitch guide

Stem Stitch

Lazy Daisy Stitch

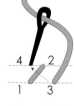

Cross Stitch

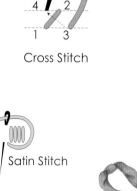

French Knot

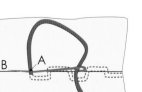

Blind Stitch

Blanket Stitch

Satin Stitch

Daisy Template

binding the quilt

1. Trim batting and backing to ¼" beyond raw edge of quilt top. This will add fullness to binding.

2. Fold and press binding strips in half lengthwise with wrong sides together.

3. Measure quilt through center from side to side. Cut two binding strips to this measurement. Lay binding strips on top and bottom edges of quilt top with raw edges of binding and quilt top aligned. Sew through all layers, ¼" from quilt edge. Press binding away from quilt top.

4. Measure quilt through center from top to bottom, including binding just added. Cut two binding strips to this measurement and sew to sides through all layers, including binding just addded. Press.

5. Folding top and bottom first, fold binding around to back then repeat with sides. Press and pin in position. Hand stitch binding in place.

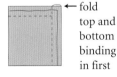

← fold top and bottom binding in first

finishing pillows

1. Layer batting between pillow top and lining. Baste. Hand or machine quilt as desired, unless otherwise indicated. Trim batting and lining even with raw edge of pillow top.

2. Narrow hem one long edge of each backing piece by folding under ¼" to wrong side. Press. Fold under ¼" again to wrong side. Press. Stitch along folded edge.

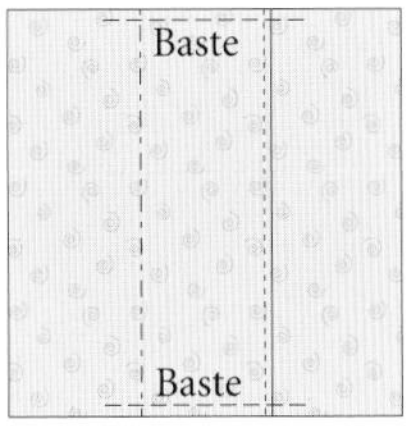

Baste

Baste

3. With right sides up, lay one backing piece over second piece so hemmed edges overlap, making single backing panel the same measurement as the pillow top. Baste backing pieces together at top and bottom where they overlap.

4. With right sides together, position and pin pillow top to backing. Using ¼"-wide seam, sew around edges, trim corners, turn right side out, and press.

pillow forms

Cut two Pillow Form fabrics to finished size of pillow plus ½". Place right sides together, aligning raw edges. Using ¼"-wide seam, sew around all edges, leaving 4" opening for turning. Trim corners and turn right side out. Stuff to desired fullness with polyester fiberfill and hand-stitch opening closed.

metric equivalency chart

inches to mm			yds to meters	
inches	mm	cm	yards	meters
⅛	3	0.3	⅛	0.11
¼	6	0.6	⅙	0.15
½	13	1.3	¼	0.23
⅝	16	1.6	⅜	0.34
¾	19	1.9	½	0.46
⅞	22	2.2	⅝	0.57
1	25	2.5	¾	0.69
1¼	32	3.2	⅞	0.80
1½	38	3.8	1	0.91
1¾	44	4.4	1⅛	1.03
2	51	5.1	1¼	1.14
2½	64	6.4	1⅜	1.26
3	76	7.6	1½	1.37
3½	89	8.9	1⅝	1.49
4	102	10.2	1¾	1.60
4½	114	11.4	1⅞	1.71
5	127	12.7	2	1.83
6	152	15.2	2⅛	1.94
7	178	17.8	2¼	2.06
8	203	20.3	2⅜	2.17
9		22.9	2½	2.29
10		25.4	2⅝	2.40
12		30.5	2¾	2.51
13		33.0	2⅞	2.63
14		35.6	3	2.74
15		38.1	3⅛	2.86
16		40.6	3¼	2.97
17		43.2	3⅜	3.09
18		45.7	3½	3.20
19		48.3	3⅝	3.31
20		50.8	3¾	3.43
21		53.3	3⅞	3.54
22		55.9	4	3.66
23		58.4	4⅛	3.77
24		61.0	4¼	3.89
25		63.5	4⅜	4.00
26		66.0	4½	4.11
27		68.6	4⅝	4.23
28		71.1	4¾	4.34
29		73.7	4⅞	4.46
30		76.2	5	4.57
36		91.4	5⅛	4.69
42		106.7	5¼	4.80
			5⅜	4.91
			5½	5.03
1 meter = 39⅜"			5⅝	5.14
			5¾	5.26
			5⅞	5.37
			6	5.49

discover more from debbie mumm®

Here's a sampling of the many quilting and home décor books by Debbie Mumm®. These books are available at your local quilt shop, by calling (888) 819-2923, or by shopping online at www.debbiemumm.com.

**Debbie Mumm's®
Cozy Northwest Christmas**
112-page, soft cover

**Debbie Mumm's®
Quilts from a Gardener's Journal**
112-page, soft cover

New!
Debbie's latest books feature enclosed wire binding so instructions and templates lay flat!

Quilting Through the Year with Debbie Mumm®
80-page, soft cover

**Debbie Mumm's®
Floral Inspirations**
80-page, soft cover

**Debbie Mumm®
Salutes America the Beautiful**
32-page, soft cover

**Debbie Mumm®
Celebrates The Holidays at Home**
80-page, soft cover

**Debbie Mumm's®
12 Days of Christmas**
140-page, soft cover

**Debbie Mumm®
Quilts Santa's Scrapbook**
112-page, soft cover

Book titles limited to stock on hand.
Products may be discontinued at any time by Debbie Mumm, Inc.

Debbie Mumm, Inc.
1116 E. Westview Court
Spokane, WA 99218

Toll Free (888) 819-2923
(509) 466-3572
Fax (509) 466-6919

www.debbiemumm.com

credits

designs by Debbie Mumm®

Special thanks to my creative teams:

editorial & project design

Carolyn Ogden: Managing Editor
Georgie Gerl: Quilt and Craft Designer
Carolyn Lowe: Quilt and Craft Designer
Laura M. Reinstatler: Writer/Editor
Maggie Bullock: Copy Editor
Jackie Saling: Craft Designer
Nancy Kirkland: Seamstress/Quilter
Wanda Jeffries: Machine Quilter
Pam Clarke: Machine Quilter

book design & production

Mya Brooks: Production Director
Tom Harlow: Graphics Manager
Heather Hughes: Graphic Designer
Nancy Hanlon: Graphic Designer
Robert H. Fitzner: Graphic Designer
Kathy Rickel: Art Studio Assistant

photography

Peter Hassel Photography
Debbie Mumm® Graphics Studio

art team

Lou McKee: Senior Artist/Designer
Kathy Arbuckle: Artist/Designer
Sandy Ayars: Artist
Heather Butler: Artist
Kathy Eisenbarth: Artist
Gil-Jin Foster: Artist

The Debbie Mumm® Sewing Studio exclusively uses Bernina® sewing machines.

special thanks

To Terri and Rick Mains for allowing us to use their French Country kitchen for on-location photography.

©2003 Debbie Mumm®
Printed in Hong Kong